To the men and women thirsty for the strength Christ's love can bring, Dale Evans Rogers tells her own extraordinary story of confusion, tragedy, enlightenment and enduring faith.

Mrs. Rogers takes her title from a passage in the Gospel according to John. A woman of Samaria meets Jesus at a well, where she has gone to draw water. Jesus asks for a drink of water and, in return, will give the woman living water. The woman asks how.

"Jesus answered and said unto her, Whosoever drinketh of this water shall thirst again: But whosoever drinketh of the water that I shall give him shall never thirst; but the water that I shall give him shall be in him a well of water springing up into everlasting life. The woman saith unto him, Sir, give me this water, that I thirst not . . ."

THE WOMAN AT THE WELL

by Dale Evans Rogers

The Woman at the Well

Dale Evans Rogers

BANTAM BOOKS
TORONTO · NEW YORK · LONDON

A NATIONAL GENERAL COMPANY

THE WOMAN AT THE WELL

*A Bantam Book / published by arrangement with
Fleming H. Revell Company*

PRINTING HISTORY
*Revell edition published April 1970
14 printings through March 1972*
Condensation in GRIT *Newspaper published June 1970*
Condensation in DETROIT NEWS SUNDAY SUPPLEMENT *published
July 1970*
Pinebrook Book Club selection published July 1970
*Christian Herald's Family Book Shelf selection published
September 1970*
*Good Housekeeping Book Club alternate selection published
May 1971*
Word Book Club selection published June 1971
Guideposts Book Club selection published April 1972
Bantam edition published June 1972

Front cover photograph by Vince Conti

Scripture quotations in this book are from the
King James Version of the Bible

*The lines from the song "You've Got to Cross That Lonesome
Valley." Copyright 1949 by G. Schirmer, Inc. Used by permission.*

Published simultaneously in the United States and Canada

PRINTED IN THE UNITED STATES OF AMERICA

And he must needs go through Samaria. Then cometh he to a city of Samaria, which is called Sychar, near to the parcel of ground that Jacob gave to his son Joseph. Now Jacob's well was there. Jesus therefore, being wearied with his journey, sat thus on the well: and it was about the sixth hour. There cometh a woman of Samaria to draw water: Jesus saith unto her, Give me to drink. (For his disciples were gone away unto the city to buy meat.) Then saith the woman of Samaria unto him, How is it that thou, being a Jew, asketh drink of me, which am a woman of Samaria? for the Jews have no dealings with the

Samaritans. Jesus answered and said unto her, If thou knewest the gift of God, and who it is that saith to thee, Give me to drink; thou wouldst have asked of him, and he would have given thee living water. The woman saith unto him, Sir, thou hast nothing to draw with, and the well is deep: from whence then hast thou that living water? Art thou greater than our father Jacob, which gave us the well, and drank thereof himself, and his children, and his cattle? Jesus answered and said unto her, Whosoever drinketh of this water shall thirst again: But whosoever drinketh of the water that I shall give him shall never thirst; but the water that I shall give him shall be in him a well of water springing up into everlasting life. The woman saith unto him, Sir, give me this water, that I thirst not . . . (John 4:4–15).

Prologue

The Bible tells us that we are always to be ready to give reason for the hope that is within us. The greatest joy and privilege of my life has been to do just that—to give my personal Christian testimony wherever and whenever it seemed good or necessary. Especially since *Angel Unaware,* the little book about our retarded baby, was published in the spring of 1953, I have been witnessing to the saving grace and power of Jesus Christ in my life, to literally thousands of people. I was sadly conscious of all the people I could not reach with these spoken testimonies. Time and working schedules made it impossible for me to accept all of the warm and wonderful invitations I have had to speak of my faith.

Hence this book, which has a double purpose: it is intended to be my autobiography, but I am more anxious to have it be my Christian witness.

It is astounding to me that so many people do not understand the meaning of "Christian witness" and "Christian testimony." A dear friend once asked me, "How can you stand up there in front of all those people and flay yourself in such a personal way?" My answer was and is, "I, personally, do not count, for my life is crucified with Christ. He counts, and I 'flay' myself only that others may see what He has done for me."

In the telling, I must be as honest as I know how to be, without embarrassing others with whom I have been concerned or involved. There have been many experiences in my life, from ages seventeen to thirty-five, which have burned deeply and left scars on me and possibly on others. Many were self-inflicted, due to the bitter disillusionment of my first marriage. Had I turned when that marriage failed, in submission to God, and had I asked Him *then* to take over my messed-up life, things might have been vastly different. Instead, I made a pact with and within myself that never again would anyone hurt me, that I would be completely independent of everybody, asking no quarter, and that *on my own* I would reach the top rung of the ladder of success and insure my own future.

Little did I realize that the only security worth fighting for is our spiritual security in Christ!

Out of respect for the feelings of others, I shall not go into detail about the many mistakes I made in my attempt to find the perfect husband and father for my child (after that first marriage went on the rocks). Let me say just that I failed miserably. Nothing turned out right, no matter how hard I tried. Fighting in the blindness of disillusionment, I struck out in all directions, hurting myself and often hurting others—never realizing what an emotionally immature and insecure and selfish person I was—always rationalizing my sense of guilt, always trying to justify my wrongdoing.

When I finally "came to myself" early in 1948, soon after my marriage to Roy Rogers, I asked the Lord to take over my life, and I set about making restitution wherever possible. Unfortunately, it is often impossible to make full and just restitution in such situations, and (this is excruciatingly painful) to get rid of one's guilt *only* in recognizing the fact that Christ died to relieve us of guilt. He died to cover every sin through His atonement. When neither of the partners in a marriage is committed all the way in the matter of faith, that marriage is on a precarious footing. Only when we realize that *all* have sinned and come short of the glory of God, and that it is a privilege to love and serve our mates *in the Lord,* do we have a chance for real wedded bliss. In the best of marriages there are squalls and sometimes tempests. If Christ is the head of the house, that house may creak

and shake in the storms *but it will stand!* I know
—from personal experience. The marriage will
stand even if only one partner to it is committed
to the Lord, because a committed Christian will
not only go the extra mile but go until he drops,
or is knocked out!

In the spring of 1968, my mother was in the
hospital with a fractured hip; one of her nurses
asked me, skeptically, if I had really written
Angel Unaware, or whether someone else had
ghost-written it for me. After all, she said, I was
"just an entertainer." When I told her how God
had inspired me and directed me in the writing
of that little book, she said, "OK. But being in
show business and publicly professing faith in
Jesus Christ does make you something of a spectacle to people, doesn't it? How do you feel
about being thought of as a sort of freak?"

I had to stop and count ten before I could
answer that one for, to me, there is nothing
freakish about a show person giving a witness.
I repeated to her the words of Paul in I Corinthians 4:9–10:

> . . . for we are made a spectacle unto the world
> and to angels and to men. We are fools for
> Christ's sake . . .

I am willing and privileged to be thought a fool,
or a spectacle, for His sake, if through my halt-
ing efforts one searching soul might find Him
as I searched and found, and in whom is life—
abundant!

DALE EVANS ROGERS

There was a woman at a well, one day
Near a city of Samaria, in a land far away.
There she met a Stranger,
  who changed her life that day,
For He gave her living water—from
  The Truth, the Life, the Way.
She left her waterpot, there by the well,
Ran into the city—*for she must tell*
  That she had met the Messiah at the well!

DALE EVANS ROGERS

THE WOMAN AT THE WELL

1

There have been many women at the well. I am one of them. In the spring of 1948, with a great thirst already in my heart, I went to a place called The Fountain Avenue Baptist Church seeking the Water of Life—and Life, in the Person of Jesus Christ, met me there. Let me tell you who and what I was, and why I was so thirsty.

I was born in Uvalde, Texas, just when I am not sure. It was either on October 30th or October 31st, 1912. I don't know, even yet, which day it was, and frankly I don't much care. I have settled on Halloween as my birthday, and more than once I have said to myself, "No wonder I have had so much trouble; I was born a witch!"

The confusion over the date really came to mean something when Roy Rogers, my good husband, and I were packing for a personal appearance theater tour in England—and incidentally to be with Billy Graham in the first week of his London Crusade for Christ, in 1954. The only record of my birth was an affidavit from my parents, which said that I had been born on October 31st, and I had lost that somewhere. The affidavit also said that I had been named Frances Octavia Smith. Nobody had any doubt about either the date or the name during all those years.

Imagine the shock—and the chagrin!—when I asked the vital statistics people in Austin, Texas, for a copy of my birth certificate, and was told that I had been born on October 30th, and that I had been named Lucille Wood Smith! I was speechless, and my mother was mad. Someone, she said, had made a stupid mistake. It could only have been the doctor who presided at my debut—and he had long since departed this vale of tears, so he wasn't much help. Mother was *sure* I was Frances Octavia, so Frances Octavia it has remained.

Frances had a difficult time arriving; my mother said that she had been given an anesthesia called twilight sleep, which not only anesthetized her, but her baby as well. For three days I made scarcely a sound. The doctors and the nurses were sure that I was an abnormal

2

child. When I finally came to, I made up for lost time with a racket that upset the whole hospital. Mother says I have been making myself heard ever since.

My parents lived on a farm belonging to my grandfather, near Italy, Texas. (Population, 1183 in 1950; what must it have been in 1912?) My father and my mother's brother ran a hardware store in Italy, in addition to farming (mostly cotton). I was the first grandchild in the family, which meant that I never lacked attention—and I loved *that*. I learned very early to watch for the mail man, who brought presents; when he didn't, I didn't like him any more. My mother says I was quite vain, especially when someone gave me new clothes; I pirouetted in front of the mirror, à la the greatest actress in the world. I also loved to sing; I would burst into song at the drop of a hat—anyone's hat, anytime, anywhere. At times it became embarrassing. When I was taken to church, I would swish my little skirt and more than once I broke away from my parents when the lively gospel songs were sung, and danced down the aisle of the church. On those occasions my father would escort me to the fire station next door, where a laying on of hands that had nothing to do with religion was firmly and not gently applied.

Mother played the piano in Sunday school, and took me along. I was interested more in what I was wearing and in what the other children were wearing than I was in the lesson for the day. Once after Sunday school my father asked me what I had learned about Jesus that

3

day, and still thinking of those clothes, I replied, "Oh, he wasn't there today." (There's food for thought in that! How often isn't Jesus there?)

When I was three I was told that God was going to send us a baby. I enthusiastically approved. It was decided that I was to accompany one of my aunts to Uvalde, to my grandparents' home, while mother was "busy" at the hospital. Aunt was on her way home from college at the time, and her train was to pass through Italy where it made a water stop. All dressed up in my Sunday best, I was driven to the station. I was beside myself with joy when I saw the train coming, its headlight lighting up the track and its whistle blowing like mad. Alas! It didn't stop! Someone had forgotten to tell the conductor to stop at Italy. It roared past us, and I had a fleeting glance of my aunt standing on the platform between the cars with her arms outstretched. For one agonizing second they thought of throwing me into her arms, but the train was going too fast. My face fell six feet as I watched the form of my aunt receding in the distance, and I cried nearly all night. How *dare* anyone treat me like this? (But we made it the next day to Uvalde, and I forgave everybody.)

When they brought the new baby boy home to Italy, I loved him. It wasn't long before I hated him. I can vouch for the trauma that occurs in the firstborn child in a family when the secondborn enters his world. I was being left out! All the bustling, all the whispering in low tones, and (I thought) all the love that had been lavished on *me*, as the only grandchild,

4

was now lavished on *him*. My nose went definitely out of joint. It was so awful that I decided to run away. If they didn't want me any more, OK, I could take care of myself somewhere else! I got as far as the wooded glen behind the farmhouse, where my grandmother caught up with me, switch in hand.

That should have cured me, but it didn't; they went right on pampering the baby, and I was even more convinced that nobody loved me and that all was lost. I hied myself out to the pigpen behind the barn to assuage my grief and my feeling of neglect by cuddling the litter of newly born little pigs. When they missed me, my father came; he stepped gingerly into the pen, between me and the distrustful old sow who was working up a storm and emitting grunts of disapproval. My father was terrified with fear that one of the little porkers would squeal before he could lift me away from the fiercely protective mother. Lift me he did, just in time; he hugged me in relief, and then there was more of the laying-on-of-hands business.

We moved into town, into Italy, where my father could give more time to the hardware store, and where I caught, in turn, just about all the sicknesses of childhood. I had mumps, chicken pox and the flu. I escaped measles, though my brother did not. I caught diphtheria, and it left me with a paralyzed palate. They cut something to loosen my speech, and after that they had a time trying to silence me! A huge evil-looking egg appeared on my neck (a glandular disturbance) which was lanced; the tonsils

5

came out at six. There was a sprained hip in the interim, caused by jumping off the running board of the family car while it was still in motion.

Double, double, toil and trouble! It was to stay with me all my life.

I was an extrovert, in these early days— extrovert, but also extremely sensitive. I was lucky enough to have relatives around me who understood that. I visited in their homes many times during my childhood, for my brother was afflicted with more than his share of sickness, and I was a handful that mother must have been glad to be rid of as often as possible. My aunt tells me that on one of my visits to her home, I had disobeyed her orders and run down the street to see a little friend. When I came back she locked me in solitary confinement in a clothes closet. This had never happened to me before, and I was badly frightened. Under this strange discipline, my wailing and weeping and gnashing of teeth was so bad that my aunt got into the closet with me. I suppose that didn't help the discipline very much, but as mercy and forgiveness and understanding, it registered deeply in my subconscious mind. She loved me enough to take the punishment with me. It was, I believe, Christlike mercy and understanding. He was compassionate enough to identify with us, to suffer with and for us. My aunt probably never knew it, but that's what she was doing.

My great-grandfather I remember as a crusty, unconventional and completely lovable old rebel who went his own way and stood on his own feet—no matter what. When his eyesight began to fail, he refused to be driven to prayer meetings on Wednesday nights and went it alone down the middle of the village street with his trusty cane. People laughed at him and loved him. I remember that he used to reach out with that cane and hook me around the neck. I didn't like it, but inside I had to smile with him. I'm sure that I inherited a lot of my love of fun from him, and I *know* that his non-conformity rubbed off on me—generously. Even when he was wrong, there was something delightful about his refusal to conform, or to do whatever everybody else did and expected him to do. Once, on the tracks near the railroad station, for some reason known only to God and to him, he paused right in the middle of the track in front of a train about to pull out of the station. The brakeman walked up to him and asked him please to get off the track; he refused to budge until his good friend the stationmaster came out and somehow moved him out of the way. He might have been arrested, but I think that even the threat of that would not have made him change his mind, or his ways.

I idolized my Grandfather Wood. We spent every Christmas and part of every summer with him in Uvalde, and from the start there was between us that rare spark of understanding and affection that adds such richness to life. He was old, but he never lost his youthfulness or his love for children and young people. Days after my birth when he looked at me in my crib, he said, "She will die hard, with her head up!"

That was prophetic, but he saw clearly. And he was right. Many the time adversity has struck at me and bowed my head, but from *somewhere* strength has always flowed into me to take it, and to bring the head up again.

My paternal grandparents lived in Centerville, Mississippi, in one of those big old rambling southern houses. Grandfather Smith owned a "mercantile" store in the town, in addition to a cotton plantation called Oleo. There were open Bibles in both grandparents' homes, well-worn and always open. Family prayers were as regular as the meals on the table. How grateful I am for that! And how I pity the child who doesn't have it! There's no telling how far I would have fallen, later, without this undergirding of Christian love and teaching. (Children, I think, *must* have this religious training while they are yet children because if they don't get it then, they may never get it at all; the chances are that they will not search for it at all until they get in a very bad way, and by that time it may be too late.) "Remember . . . thy creator in the days of thy youth . . ." (Ecclesiastes 12:1). As the twig is bent, so grows the tree.

My father grew up in the old home in Centerville, along with four sisters and two brothers, under a strict discipline mixed with a great amount of love. That love rubbed off from him upon everyone he knew, and it was especially strong in his family circle. His mother's (my Grandmother Smith's) health was poor when he was born, and he was nursed through infancy and into childhood by a wonderful black mam-

8

my whose parents and grandparents had been slaves on the Smith plantation. When slavery was abolished, she chose to stay with the family that her parents had served and loved—and who had been loved in return. I think my father loved Aunt Lethie almost as much as he loved his own mother. After his marriage to my mother he would go back to the old home in Mississippi for an occasional visit, and he always brought a hug and a present for Aunt Lethie. I remember the house as being full of fun and laughter and literally jumping with family, friends and neighbors. My father loved to dance—and dance he did, though it was forbidden by his (Baptist) church and family. (*Another* non-conformist!) His family was not rich, but it was what people then called "well off"—which probably meant comfortable. He was educated in (Baptist) Hillman College. (When he was born he was named Hillman for the founder of that college.)

My mother's family was Baptist, too, but something slipped somewhere, and she was graduated from Texas Presbyterian College. Her father loved music and always wanted a musician in the family, so she and her sisters were forced to study piano all through grammar, high school and college. That isn't a good way to produce a good musician, or a good anything else! Today she can hardly play a C scale, and hardly ever goes near a piano. Whatever musical talent she may have had was forced out of her. I have often heard her say, "If I was given a talent, I never found it—unless it was for washing dishes." But she *did* have a talent—the superb talent of being a good wife and mother. There was and is a great music in my mother, and it has been expressed in her ability to "train up a child in the way he should go" (Proverbs 22:6). It was a talent, almost instinctive, to instill in her children a strong sense of right and wrong and a desire to do what was right. God gave her that talent, and she has used it well.

I rebelled and drifted often from my moorings across the next twenty-five years, but that did not make her discipline wrong; nor did it diminish her love for her strong-headed little rebel, no matter what I did nor where I went. In all those turbulent, floundering years her example was always before me and her influence strong within me, no matter how much I tried to rationalize and to justify what I knew was wrong. Mother often remarked, "Frances is too impulsive; she means well, but she rushes into things before she thinks them through."

She knew me like a book—and still does. I am thankful that she does, just as I am thankful that the Lord "knoweth our frame; he remembereth that we are dust" (Psalm 103:14); and that He is always there waiting for His rebellious child to accept His mercy and forgiveness and come home. She loved me and stayed with me, regardless of my waywardness—suffering with me in my self-imposed dilemmas—keeping the faith that some day I would come to myself and back to Him. Had she lost her faith in God and in me . . . I can't even bear the thought of what might have happened to me. (This is why I go up and down the land "witnessing." I urge Christians, young and old, to be faithful to God, persevering in prayer in behalf of those they love—never despairing, never doubting that God, like a good parent, is willing and able to do abundantly more than we ask.)

When I was seven we moved to Arkansas. Father's brother had a farm in Arkansas, where they raised long staple cotton for a ready and lucrative market. He wrote, urging Dad to "come over into Macedonia" (Acts 16:9), and help work the farm and enjoy the sure-fire profits of what looked like an unusually good year. Dad was one of those men who always thought the grass was greener somewhere else, so he turned the farm in Texas back to my grandfather, sold the hardware business, and off we went to Arkansas.

It wasn't a good year. It was a year of unusually long and flooding rains, boll weevils and the worst crop ever. We lost everything, but I am still thankful for the year we lived in that small frame house; it was good experience. It was primitive, but the smell of the good earth was wonderfully pungent, and there was a big vegetable garden and plenty of fresh milk and butter—and there were playmates. Near us lived a family of tenant sharecroppers—a black family with two children near my age. We had great fun together, playing cowboys 'n Indians, and hide-and-seek, and building castles in the air. There was one firm rule laid down by our parents that we never disobeyed: we could play together outside all we wished, but that was it, and all of it. They never came into our house, and we never went into theirs; when company came we separated and shut the doors of our respective homes. We children never discussed this; we knew that it was expected of us, and we accepted it; but it was hard for me to understand why we were so different at times like these, and so much alike playing in God's out-of-doors. I finally said that it was unfair to have to separate just because company came. Dad told me, "Hush! When you're older, you will understand." I still don't!

It rained, and it rained, and it rained. The roads were impossible, knee-deep in mud and slippery even for a car with chains, so we were seldom on the road. We had no electricity in that house—only oil lamps and an oil burner for heat. My brother and I had a few toys—very few, but enough to enjoy them. I am glad for that—glad that we didn't have so many toys that we wouldn't really enjoy any of them. I found fun in simple things; my greatest kick came when I pulled a few mustard greens from the garden and cooked them on my toy iron stove. The stove smoked furiously, but the aroma was heavenly!

One dark morning a man drove up to our house and slid into the muddy front yard in a horse-drawn buggy. He handed my mother a telegram which told her that my grandmother, "Mama Wood," was critically ill in a San Antonio hospital. We left the following day. How well

I remember walking into that hospital room—I was only seven—and seeing my beloved grandmother lying there close to death. She was so pale! Her lovely iron-gray hair was piled atop her head, and she wore an expression of perfect peace and submission to whatever her Lord had in store for her. It was so clear: *she was not afraid.* She knew that she was to be on the operating table early the next morning; she didn't know that the surgeon was fearful that she couldn't survive the long operation to remove unbelievably large gallstones, and that he was afraid that peritonitis had already set in. I doubt that she would have been afraid, even if she had known. Like the Apostle Paul, she had learned to be content in whatever state she found herself.

She smiled, and asked me to rub her aching arms. As I rubbed, the nearness of her and the faith that was within her filled me with a strange new feeling of love and peace that I did not understand at the time. There were huge beads of perspiration on her serene forehead. Young as I was, I sensed that she was in pain.

My brother and I were taken to the family home in Uvalde, where we were to wait until the operation was over, and Mama Wood could come home again. Waiting there was almost as bad as it would have been in the hospital, for the shadow of death was over the place. The family talked in hushed voices of Mama and her love and her life—about how she looked up from the stretcher on which they had carried her out of the house and said with a smile, "Whatever the Lord wants, I am ready for it"; of how she had said, at the door, "Take care of my baby." Her baby was fourteen years old —my youngest aunt. She worried about that at the gates of death; I think she knew she would never come home to Uvalde. She didn't. The operation came too late, and she died two days later.

They brought her back to lie in beautiful peace in the parlor of the old Texas home. She was beautiful—so beautiful that I could not keep my eyes from her face; my mother had real difficulty keeping me from just standing beside the casket and staring at her. I can still see her today, fifty years later, sleeping so quietly, smiling faintly, in a white crepe-de-chine-and-lace dress with a wide pink satin sash and with a look of utter serenity on her face. Somewhere, recently, I read in a book or a magazine, "The two most beautiful things in life are to be seen at the extremes of life: the laughter of a child and the look of peace on the face of one who has just died in faith." That look was on her face; it was the product of long years of love. She had known the travail and trouble of a mother with seven girls and one boy, but with it all she brought them up in faith and she left her faith in their hearts. She was never demonstrative with them in her affection; it was subtle, but tremendously real and powerful. One day Grandfather said to her, "Mama, I hardly ever see you hugging and kissing the children." She said quietly, "Never mind that, Papa. Still waters run deep." The spiritual "deep" in her called unto the deep in her children; it called out the best in them—and in me.

This was my first brush with death, and it was beautiful—so beautiful that it gave me a strength to face far-distant encounters with death, of which, then, I knew nothing.

We went back to Arkansas, and life began again. I got to know my cousins better after this, and spent more time with them in their big two-story house. We wrestled with each other and chased each other up and down the great stairway in the front hall. We had a lot of fun with Liney, their boisterous, rollicking and very religious cook. Liney could neither read nor write, but the Christian faith that was in her put many a "superior" white adult and child to shame. I can still hear her singing hymns and rattling pans in the kitchen. Her favorite was my cousin Quentin, who used to read the Bible to her every day. In the evenings he would sit at the side of her bed and read the Scriptures to her, and she would nod her head and cry yes! in assent to the great truths of the Book. Many years later, after her chicks had left the house, she was found dead on her knees beside the bed; apparently she had died in prayer. What a way to go! She had a great, direct, influence on Quentin, as he grew to the status of manhood, and I know now that—indirectly—she had influence on all of us. I think of her whenever I hear someone say or sing, "No man is an island. . . ." We are *all* a part of

each other and of God; every move we make
has its influence, for good or ill.

Soon my brother and I were enrolled in
school; our first-grade teacher was Miss Blanche,
who was held in high respect by her small
charges. She loved us, and she demanded—
and received—implicit obedience. She won our
love, and the love and cooperation of our parents. How different it is today, when the kids
have so little respect for the teacher, and when
so many parents defend the misbehaving child
against the correction of the teacher! I wonder
sometimes how such a situation ever got going!

Miss Blanche had a paddle, and she *used* it.
We eyed her weapon with awe. We knew what
to expect when we sassed Miss Blanche, or
showed her any discourtesy. What's wrong with
that, anyway? Have you ever watched an old
mother bear cuff her cubs? She does it in the
interests of survival; she knows that if she
doesn't teach them the rules of bear life, they
will *die.* The same thing goes for *our* cubs! I'm
for a limited, careful, merciful use of the paddle.
We've spared the paddle too much, and the
result is that we have reared a generation of
hard-boiled, insolent youngsters who, never
having known the paddle, do not hesitate to use
a gun or a Molotov cocktail to get what they
think they want. Today we reap the whirlwind
of our lack of discipline, and we wonder why!

Miss Blanche's paddle looked—and sounded
—worse than it was. Each day she lined up the
little trespassers and applied the penalty; it was
never severe; neither was it ever forgotten. Ac-

cording to their need, they got it, some one stroke, some two, some five, but never a hundredfold. None of us, so far as I can remember, ever experienced any emotional conflicts from it, but all of us refrained from telling our parents about what teacher had done to us; we knew too well that we'd get *another* going over from them if we did. Believe you me, we were careful—and hesitant to sin in that classroom. Frances Smith was *very* careful, so she suffered few chastisements, but one day Frances stepped out of line, and was called for the lineup. Trembling in my Buster Browns, I stepped up to Miss Blanche and said in a trembling voice, "If you spank me, I'll get another spanking when I get home!" Mercy conquered justice in that good and wise teacher. She hid her laughter behind her hand and said, "All right, Frances; you deserve it, but I think you have suffered enough already," and she hung up the paddle. Heaven only knows how relieved I was that day—but today I think she did me no favor. She could have gone a little easier than usual, but she really should have spanked me. It might have helped me the next time I acted purely on impulse in getting out of line.

Since my parents had taught me my numbers and the alphabet before I entered the school, I skipped half of the first grade, all of the second, and went right into the third grade. I think that was wrong, too. Children are children for such a short time! We can skip too much, in human experience—skip too many valuable experiences. My mother felt the same way about it. She used to say that I was "born grown" (born more mature than most) since I always seemed to prefer the company of those who were older than I.

All in all, I loved school; I was a good student (which was good) and I knew it (which was bad). I also loved music, so I started taking piano lessons when I was eight years old. It went well for a time, until I began to get impatient with scales and with those everlasting exercises, and began to improvise and to play the way *I* wanted it! The little rebel on the piano stool produced improvisations that nearly drove her poor teacher out of her mind and finally, in anger and despair, she said bluntly that I was wasting her time and that my parents were wasting their money—and stalked out. It was too bad; Paderewski was getting old, and I might have succeeded him as the world's greatest pianist. As it turned out, I played thereafter only by ear, and only well enough to play simple hymns in Sunday school. So I turned to voice and I sang my first solo at a worship service in the church. It was "In the Garden" accompanied by the organist.

Friday nights I spent in the homes of my girl friends, or they spent the night in ours. Saturdays were given to straightening out dresser drawers and helping with the household chores. Sundays we went to Sunday school, to church services and the meetings of the Baptist Young Peoples' Union. There was an evangelistic service at 7:30 in the evening, and I was expected to be there, too. All this was not so much demanded as expected, and it never occurred to me to goof off on any of it until I reached my early teens. Then the usual generation gap became evident. (We talk of the generation gap as though it were something new. It isn't. It has *always* been there!)

Our church nearly disbanded while I was still going to BYPU; there was a marital scandal that tore the place apart. I was badly upset by it, and so were all the others; it took years to rebuild the faith and confidence of the whole membership. An almost desperate attempt was made to hush-hush the whole business; the older members just didn't want the young people—like me—to know anything about it (which of course was silly), lest they get the idea that there were anything but 100-percent-perfect Christians in the church. It's too bad that such scandals happen in such places; it's also too bad that we tend to put Christians on pedestals, and that we refuse to acknowledge that we *all* have feet of clay. That goes for the best of them. Of course it is no small thing for a Christian to fall into grievous sin, but it seems to me a greater sin to refuse to get up out of the ditch through repentance and confession and restitution. The rest of us must continue in faith in the presence of such sin and scandal and go on behaving like Christians. Too many Christians are fringe Christians, people-watchers instead of Christ-watchers. We need to remember Christ's words about sinning in thought as well as in deed—and to remember that none of us can stand spotless. If more of that spirit had been present in that congregation at that time, it would not have been so traumatic—especially for me. It took a long time to get over it.

Church and school were quite close in those days; what we learned in one carried over into the other. Each school day, for instance, began with a short prayer. We had school chapel every Friday morning, to which different ministers from all the churches in town brought a short talk; we called it "the sermon." It was tremendously effective. There were children in that school whose parents never darkened the door of any church—but there were seeds planted in their children, those Friday mornings, that blossomed and flowered into fine Christian character in later days. I loved it; we all loved it. I still believe it was good, and I think it was a tragic mistake in American education to make any religious emphasis illegal in the schoolroom. How could we be so blind and apathetic as to permit one atheist to bar prayer from the schools? Our children need this God-given power in their lives, if they are to survive in today's jungle of desperate, vicious, dog-eat-dog existence.

If this sounds harsh, let's face it: we are living in times when every decent anchor we have known on the sea of life is being cut loose or thrown overboard, leaving us helplessly adrift. Is it any wonder that we have so much tragedy in the lives of our confused youngsters? The basic needs of these youngsters have not changed. The same situations have occurred in generation after generation—only to different people. Young people have always been self-centered; they have always thought that *their* generation was the only one to experience the growing pains of maturity. They are always surprised to discover that their parents *do* understand their problems. This is one reason why I have faith in this generation. In spite of us, in spite of themselves, they will mature into adults able to cope with their world—*if* we parents and grandparents do everything we can to preserve human freedom and the right to worship the eternal God Who guaranteed this right and freedom in His Word, the Holy Bible.

When I was ten, an itinerant evangelist came to town and our church had a revival. Again I heard the old, old story of Jesus and His love —but this time it was presented in such a dramatic and straightforward way that it really shook me up. That evangelist opened the gates of hell and I had a good look at it; I was so thoroughly frightened at the prospect of spending eternity in such a miserable and terrifying place that I reached out desperately for the hand of the Saviour. I *reached,* but I did not *dedicate.* I reached, in fear, but I was not really ready to hand over control of my life to Him. I was like a child who cannot swim but who wants to learn in the ocean all by himself: he asks his father, an experienced swimmer, to stand on the shore and, if the waves overpower him, to jump in and save him. I thought I'd like to have God nearby, if I got into trouble, but . . . ! I made my way down the aisle of the church and stretched out my hand to Jesus

Christ. In honest and complete truth, it was no soul-shaking experience; it was only a matter of laying hold upon eternal security. A few weeks later I was baptized by immersion, and then I felt that I really had it made. Not for years did it occur to me that what I had done was not enough—that in addition to this faith in Christ to save me from peril and even from death, I had to turn over my whole life to Him—to be used as He saw fit.

Furthermore, being gregarious, aggressive and self-assertive, and with a consuming zest for colorful adventure, I still had the notion that God might hold me back from something I wanted to do on my own. With such an attitude, my spiritual life hardly got off the ground, in spite of my march down the aisle! True, I read my Sunday school lessons and the BYPU materials, but that was about it—about *all* of it. I never thought of really seeking the Lord, and more often than not I would fall asleep at night repeating the Lord's Prayer with no thought at all of really talking with Him about the questions that bothered me and about the guilty feeling I had about my questionable thoughts and behavior. I just didn't give myself a chance to know the One who cared most about me and my future.

At eleven, I discovered that I had nerves. Because of overwork in school due to my skipping the seventh grade and participating in too many extra-curricular activities, I had a nervous breakdown, plus a spot on a lung. I spent the whole summer vacation in bed. I had tried to do more than my physical body could take, and I had to pay the piper in enforced idleness.

As an adolescent, boys had fascinated me, as they fascinate most adolescent girls. My family often laughed at my performances with the boys, and that stung me; I was oversensitive to ridicule of any sort, and I wanted to grow up quickly. I was *sure* I was old enough to do what I was doing. My parents tried to stem this feeling, so that I could enjoy my childhood as long as possible, and I resented that and began to strain at the leash. There were public dances at the courthouse attended by "everybody in town," and I cajoled my mother into accompanying me to those dances as one of the mother-chaperons for younger girls who were too young to date. I loved dancing, though it was frowned upon by our church, so I went to the courthouse hops, and before long I was dancing every dance. Here I met my first steady —a boy from a neighboring town.

He was quite handsome, and in his late teens. I was fourteen. We went everywhere together —to the dances, to parties, everywhere. Poor Mother couldn't stop it, even when she realized that it was getting out of hand. She forbade me to see him—but I still saw him. Had I really known what the honor-thy-father-and-thy-mother commandment meant, I would have stopped; as it was, rebellion flared inside me and I met the boy secretly at the homes of friends. Came the night when I was supposed to be at a play rehearsal and spending the night with a girl friend—we eloped. He had obtained a marriage license that afternoon in the Gretna Green of our area, lying about his age and mine. We drove to his town, were married in the home of a minister and sped away across the line into Tennessee to his mother's home, where we spent the weekend.

I knew that my parents would be frantic, and I was conscience-stricken at the heartbreak I had caused them. I called my mother long-distance, and told her I was married. Never will I forget the awful, throbbing silence that followed, but it didn't last long. She forgave me and asked us to come home. We went home the next day; he went to work for his father, and we moved in with his father and step-mother.

My mother pleaded with me to go back to high school, since I was in the junior class and would graduate in another year. I refused. All I wanted, then, was to be a good wife and to start a home of my own.

The marriage turned out to be a dismal failure —but God sent me a son who did not become a failure. My boy Tom was to become the shining light of my life. He seemed so much like the little boy Samuel, in the Bible—quiet, thoughtful, bright. When he was six months old his father announced that our marriage had been a mistake, that he was too young to be tied down with a wife and baby, and that he wanted a divorce. I loved him, and I pleaded with him to give our marriage a chance, but—no!

My blessed mother said she would help me

raise the boy, and help me get on my feet as a provider. I knew that I would have to do most of it myself, so to prepare myself for a business career I enrolled in a business school. Because of my good grades in high school, the business school accepted me without a high school diploma—at the age of sixteen and a half.

My days were busy enough, but at night I was lonely and I wept a sea of tears before applying for a divorce a year later. The court awarded me complete custody of our son on grounds of desertion. I asked no support from Tom's father. My pride had been trampled in the dust, and I wanted nothing from him, nothing, ever again.

2

We moved to Memphis, and that was good for me. It was a change of scene—new environment, new friends, new activities. I started attending church regularly now, singing in the choir and working in various church groups in the effort to forget. For the first time I read the Bible from cover to cover. I found much that I could not understand, but what I did understand I made a real effort to retain. I was still in my teens.

Mother looked out for Tom as though he were *her* child! Once she suggested that she adopt him legally, since I was still so young—and so busy. I couldn't bring myself to do that, even for my dear mother. Tom called her Mom and he called me Sassie; he still couldn't pronounce Frances.

My first job after business school was with a bus company in Memphis. I was there just three weeks when I was offered another job, as a secretary in an insurance firm. It was a good job, and I grabbed it, but I was more interested in show business than I was in the insurance business. I spent a great deal of time singing and accompanying myself on the piano. I also wanted to write short stories. I did write several—all flops. They all came back from the publishers accompanied by the dreaded rejection slip. It dawned on me that millions would never read me as they read O. Henry, so I tried song writing. This was easier. I wrote several that were just plain terrible, and then one that I thought was good enough to submit to a music publisher. I submitted it in person, sang it in the publisher's office and was flattered by a vague promise that they would consider it. For several months I waited—while they considered; one day I was in a music store and I heard my tune, slightly altered, on a phonograph record bearing the name of another composer.

As I said, nothing was turning out right for me. As I look back at it now, I think of that great and profound truth in Francis Thompson's poem, *The Hound of Heaven:* "All things betrayeth thee who betrayest Me." It was really happening.

One day I sat at my desk in the insurance

office staring vaguely at an accident claim form in my typewriter. Actually I was trying to think up words to fit a tune I had just composed, when the boss walked in. He stood there looking at me for a moment, and then he exploded, "Young lady, I think you are in the wrong business!" My fingers flew to the keyboard and I typed like a maniac. He walked away, turned, came back to me, and said, "How would you like to sing on a radio program?" The heavens opened! Bells rang and trumpets sounded! *Would* I? He asked me if I could accompany myself on the piano; if I could, he might just get me on as a guest on a radio program in which he had a sponsor's interest.

The next Friday night Frances Fox made her radio debut, playing and singing "Mighty Lak a Rose." In those days you were permitted to dedicate your song to anyone you chose, and so my first dedication—the first of many to come—was to my son Tommy. Someone must have liked it for they offered me a regular spot at the radio station.

I held onto the secretarial job; radio offered only experience but with no pay. How I loved it! Civic organizations in town began inviting me to sing at luncheons and banquets. Once in a while I got paid for these appearances in real money (as much as twenty dollars); mostly I was paid in chicken croquettes and peas. The experience was good. I learned to meet and face the public, and within a few months' time I had moved up from that first small radio station to the most powerful one in Memphis.

When the big dance bands came to town I would go with an escort to hear them, and sometimes I would be asked to sing a number with the orchestra, using a big, old-fashioned megaphone. My name began to get up there in popular demand. I reasoned that if I could crack Memphis, I could crack Chicago, and off I rushed to subdue the Windy City.

I didn't crack Chicago; it cracked me. After a few short years I wound up with a case of severe anemia due to overwork as a secretary. Nothing worked—no matter how hard I tried. I just couldn't make the grade. Finally, with my money gone and my health broken, I wired my folks for money enough to get home. My parents had moved back to Texas and were living on a farm. We were a miserable pair, Tommy and I, as we rode the train back to Texas. After two weeks in the hospital and much intake of liver and iron, I was released for three months' rest on the farm.

In the fall of that same year I landed a job in Louisville, Kentucky—my first job with really good pay. The program director at Station WHAS there gave me my professional name, Dale Evans, when I joined the staff. It was designed primarily for the ease of announcers (it rolls off the tongue easily), and is almost impossible to mispronounce or misspell. (And, I might add, it stuck!)

Tommy went with me, just as he had gone with me to Chicago, but he didn't stay. I came home from work one day and the lady who was caring for him told me that he had been vomiting all day, and that he had severe pains in his legs and arms. I was nearly frantic with fear; there was an epidemic of infantile paralysis raging in Kentucky. In agony I prayed when they took Tommy to the hospital for a spinal tap. I promised God, tearfully, that I would put Him first in my life if Tom's test proved to be negative. It was negative, and for a few weeks I prayed and read my Bible every day, but . . . my musical ambition was too strong—stronger than my spiritual devotion, and strong enough to make me forget my promise to God. Back to Texas and the farm we went, beaten again!

My boy loved that farm, and the small community life surrounding it. The first day there he chased the poor hens all over the place, until both he and the chickens dropped from sheer exhaustion. His cheeks bloomed with health, and for the first time I was secure in the knowledge that he was safe and happy.

But I still had to find work—somewhere. I couldn't let my parents do it all. I found a job singing on the staff of Station WFAA, in Dallas, on the Early Bird program; I also found a husband. One day in Dallas I had a long-distance call from a pianist and orchestral arranger with whom I had worked in Louisville. We had dated frequently there, but when we said good-by I never expected to see him again. He said he was on his way to make a fortune in California and intended to stop over in Dallas. If he could find work there, he might stay awhile before going on to the Coast. He was offered a job playing piano and arranging for the staff band at WFAA in Dallas, and our dates began and multiplied. A year later we were married.

Two years later I found myself back in Chicago with my musician husband. ("She'll die hard, with her head up!") My dreams *did* die hard.

I registered with several booking agencies in Chicago, and auditioned like mad. One audition finally paid off: I was engaged as a jazz singer with an orchestra at the Edgewater Beach Hotel. It was a step up, but not too pleasant a step. Another girl did all the pretty ballads and got most of the applause; the Edgewater was a dignified ballroom, and jazz wasn't popular there. It was tough.

Anson Weeks' orchestra was playing at the Aragon Ballroom at the time, and he was looking for a female vocalist. I was hired. For the next year I sang on the proverbial dance band one-nighters and hotel engagements, driving hundreds of miles from date to date. I finally left the band so that I could have Tom with me; he was now ready for junior high school. A job opened on the staff of WBBM (CBS network); I auditioned, and got it. At the same time I sang every night at the Blackstone, Sherman and Drake hotels, and I made it to the top spot—the then famous Chez Paree Supper Club. Things did seem to be picking up, at last.

I went to church regularly now with Tom; I wanted him to have what I would not take for myself—a solid relationship with the Lord. The minister was a bit disturbing. Every now and then he would say something about "the claims of Jesus Christ," and I would feel myself drawn toward the Cross. After the church services were over, I would rationalize again my feelings of guilt for not making a definite stand for Christ and for not following His commandments. I would reckon that the Lord might demand something that would cost more than I could pay—that He might ask something that would jeopardize my precious career. I wanted nothing that would deter me from making a name for myself in show business—from making a lot of money and being independent and in a position to guarantee a good future for Tom by way of college or in whatever he wanted to do. One part of me wanted to be married and a good housekeeper and mother, and the other part wanted to be an entertainer. It was like trying to ride two horses at once and not being able to control either one of them.

Suddenly, right out of the blue, I got a telegram from an agent in Hollywood who had heard me sing on a broadcast that reached California. I laughed long and loud when I read it. He asked for photographs of me. If he liked the photographs, he would arrange a screen test for me. Me! I had no desire whatever to go to Hollywood; I was aiming at musical comedy in New York, thank you, and besides, I did not think I was pretty enough to be in pictures. I wasn't an actress—and I was twenty-eight years old. So I ignored the telegrams which kept coming. Finally, I took them to my program director who said that I should give it a whirl.

Still laughing and still not believing in it, I had the inevitable glamour photos taken, and sent the best of them to the agent, Mr. Rivkin, in Hollywood.

He wired me to take a plane immediately for a screen test at Paramount Studios. And I did.

My heart was pounding fast, as I boarded the sleeping plane for Hollywood. It was my first long flight. I had never crossed the country in a plane before, and I got an earache ten feet off the ground and suffered with it all night long. (In those days, there was no adjustable pressure system to compensate for high altitudes.) The stewardess dropped warm oil in my ears, but it didn't help much. I couldn't eat any breakfast because of nausea, and as the plane started descent for the landing in Burbank I wished with all my heart that I could have been anywhere but *there*. I wished I had never heard of any Hollywood agent, but I had to meet him. Lucky for me, I thought, that I can wear dark glasses to hide the ravages of the painful night. I looked out of my window and saw a man pacing up and down, looking nervously at the plane. This had to be the one. I'd read in a book that all agents were nervous.

I got down the steps to the ground somehow; I'll never know how. I walked over to him and quavered, "Are you Joe Rivkin?"

He stopped pacing, stood there with an incredulous look on his face, sized me up (and down) and he said, "My God! Are *you* Dale Evans?" I never felt so put down in my life!

I said, "Oh, Mr. Rivkin, I had a terrible night."
He didn't seem to hear it. He kept staring, and
suddenly he spoke again.

"Take off those glasses!"

I pulled them off as slowly as possible; he
caught his breath, and turned pale. Finally he
said, "Well, you don't look like your pictures!"
I wanted to run back into the plane and take
off for almost anywhere in the world but Hollywood. What a welcome!

I thought the worst of it was over as we piled
into his car, baggage and all, and started down
the road for Hollywood. Then looking down he
saw the wedding ring on my finger, and
howled: "You didn't tell me you were married."

"You didn't ask me."

Silence. A long, stabbing silence.

"How old are you?"

I had been told to say that I was twenty-two.
I said that.

"No," he said. "You are twenty-one. Got it?
And you are *single*. Understand?"

I understood, and I didn't like it. I didn't like
the whole set-up. I didn't even answer him, but
in my mind I had decided to go through the
screen test, enjoy the vacation, see Hollywood
and then get back to Chicago and resume my
musical career. I was sure that nothing would
develop from this venture in the flicks.

He drove like he wanted to get nowhere fast,
and from time to time he looked me up and
down and he seemed more disgusted every time
he looked. I got the idea that he didn't like anything about me, but I held my chin up and

35

pretended to be enjoying the scenery—which I wasn't.

"I don't like your lipstick. Don't wear it any more. I don't like your hair, either. We'll have to do something about it." Sure enough, when we reached the Hollywood Plaza Hotel he rushed me downstairs to the beauty salon, introduced me to an operator and said, "See what you can do with her. And step on it. We have to be at Paramount in an hour." I felt like a prize pig being groomed for exhibition at a small-town fair. I didn't care what might happen at Paramount. All I wanted was a little rest.

The operator gave me a stinging facial massage. ("Get a little blood in that face," Rivkin told her.) She tinted my light brown hair with auburn rinse, and sent me off to dress for a luncheon with a Mr. Meiklejohn, a casting director at Paramount. Now, for luncheon in Chicago, a dark dress with furs and gloves was the proper thing, so I put on a sheer dark dress, selected a fur (my *only* fur!), pulled on a pair of spotless white gloves and walked into the lobby with all the pride and confidence of Cleopatra on her barge. Rivkin saw me coming, and he put his hands over his eyes.

"Who's dead?" he asked, "your agent? What's the black dress for?" I could have popped him, then and there, but for once I kept control of my temper, and replied haughtily, à la Cleopatra, "In Chicago, sir, this is proper dress for a business meeting at noon."

"Well, you're not in Chicago now. You're in Hollywood, and in Hollywood you wear bright colors, with flowers—casual. But it's too late now. Come on!" By the time we reached the office of the casting director, I was shaking like a leaf, inside and outside.

Mr. Meiklejohn was gentle and kind as we smiled at each other and shook hands. He said, "Dale, you remind me a lot of my wife when she first came to Hollywood." I liked that, and I liked him. He took my arm and led me through the maze of people in the dining room; they all stopped eating and craned their necks to see "the new one." I wished the floor would open and swallow me up—away from those eyes. At the table, I felt like a tennis ball in a very fast game.

"Dale," Mr. Meiklejohn asked, "how old are you?"

"Twenty-one," shouted Joe Rivkin. The director looked long and hard at my face, and then he said, "I'm a little worried about the nose. A trifle too long for the chin." I felt like saying that the good Lord had given me the nose, and if he didn't mind, I'd keep it, but I never had the chance to say anything. Rivkin beat me to it with, "Don't worry about the nose; we'll have some of it taken off."

Mr. Meiklejohn: "Dale, do you dance?"

Mr. Rivkin: "Dance? She makes Eleanor Powell look like a bum!"

Miss Evans: "No, I can't dance, Mr. Meiklejohn. I can't even do a time step." I explained that I had turned down a chance at a part in the stage musical, "Hold Onto Your Hats" because I was not a professional dancer. I could do ballroom well enough, but not solo.

Bill Meiklejohn almost blew his top when he heard that. He looked at Joe Rivkin with an icy stare that would have frozen a polar bear into silence, reminded him in a few well-chosen words that his ancestry was in doubt and that he was suspicious of the whole deal. But Joe wasn't frozen; he promised quickly and glibly that I could pick up the dancing in no time at all.

The director turned to me and explained that I had been summoned for a screen test with an eye to the ingenue lead in the picture *Holiday Inn*, starring Bing Crosby and Fred Astaire. They were looking for a new (female) personality for the picture, but since I could not dance, they would make the screen test anyway, and perhaps something might come of it. Whereupon the luncheon ended and I was taken to the wardrobe department and introduced to Miss Edith Head, who fitted me out with a dress and a fur muff formerly worn by Barbara Stanwyck. Then the dramatic coach took me under his wing. He picked a scene from Marlene Dietrich's picture, *Blue Angel*, and told me that MacDonald Carey was to play opposite me.

I worked hard all that week and the next. Joe Rivkin watched me like a hawk watching a chicken; he saw to it that I did not stay out late and that I had plenty of time to study my part in the test. He also told me what I could and could not eat, in the interests of reducing my weight. I was getting more and more nervous about the whole business—particularly about the deception with my age, and about the fact that I had a son.

The day of the screen test I was carefully made up and gowned, and taken to the set by my agent. As I sat there waiting for the crew to get the lights set up, a sense of doubt and shame swept over me. Basically I was completely honest about it all, but I hated any form of deception, and I knew that all this was not on the up-and-up. I felt as though I would blow up under the tension. I got up and walked over to Joe Rivkin and told him that I must talk to him, alone and *right now,* before things went further. We walked out into the alley behind the studio; I turned and faced him like a cornered criminal and I said, "Mr. Rivkin, I have not been completely honest with you, and I can't go on with this thing until you know the facts. I am not twenty-one; I am twenty-eight. I have a son who is twelve years old. He lives with me."

His jaw dropped as though he had been clobbered with a meat-ax. He paced up and down muttering, "Let me think, let me think." Suddenly he had the solution:

"You will have to send him away to school."

That seemed to make it worse than ever. I refused, saying that if Tom could not come to Hollywood with me, we would stay in Chicago. I could make a good living in Chicago, and my husband, who was well-placed in Chicago radio, would add to my security. Biting his nails, Rivkin tried another tack.

"Tom is your brother. Do you understand?"

I still didn't like it, but at least it gave me the chance to have Tom with me in Hollywood and that was something. So I said, "All right. It's all right with me if it's all right with Tom." It was all right with Tom. (He commented, "It sounds pretty silly, but you can do anything you want, Mother, as long as I myself don't have to lie.") I figured that with what I could make on a good Hollywood job I could send him to college and give him the musical education he so desperately wanted. Besides, my husband wanted to come to Hollywood to compose, orchestrate and score films, and that would be all to the good.

Rivkin reckoned that it would all work out —*if* I would just keep my mouth shut about having a husband and a child. In my heart I knew it was wrong, but again I rationalized. Nothing would come of the screen test, anyway, so why worry?

I took the test, and flew home to Chicago to wait it out. Actually, I was still hankering for a place in a New York stage show, so I didn't worry too much. I had almost put Hollywood out of my mind when I got a call from Mr. Rivkin, who told me (excitedly) that while Paramount had not taken up their option on me, Twentieth Century Fox had bought me at a salary of four hundred dollars per week on a one-year contract.

It looked like a lot of money, after all our lean years. We (the whole family) talked it over and over and over, and decided that we should give it a whirl. I packed.

3

Mother, Tom and I flew to Los Angeles, leaving my husband behind to work out his contract with the NBC studios in Chicago. He and his parents, who were living with us at the time, followed us a month later. We rented a house in West Los Angeles. I put on my best bib and tucker and checked in at Twentieth Century Fox for work. I was told to get ready for another screen test. Actually, *they* got me ready.

I was sent to a dentist to have my teeth capped and levelled; I was hustled off to a health club to get rid of some weight. I was pummeled, pounded, massaged, steamed and exercised until the scales reported that I had lost twelve pounds, which seemed to satisfy them—at least for the moment. Then they produced the dramatic coach of the studios—Tom Moore of the old silent film era, and a most kindly man. For the test he chose a reading of selections from *The Hound of Heaven*, by Francis Thompson. I wondered why. He said there was a spiritual quality in my face, and he wanted to project that in the test. He must have been a very perceptive and sensitive soul—a lot more perceptive and sensitive than I was. I wasn't even dimly aware of any such quality either in my face or in my heart, and no one else I had ever known had noticed it, so far as I knew. How ironic that he should choose that masterpiece! I could barely understand who the Hound of Heaven was, much less read it with any depth of feeling. Years later, after I had found God and Christ, someone sent me a copy of *The Hound of Heaven*, and this time I understood it perfectly. I saw that it told my own story of running and hiding from the Hound (God) over eighteen years of sunshine and shadow, toil and pleasure, success and defeat, trying hard to get out of my ears and out of my life the sound of those steady, strong haunting feet that followed me everwhere.

The studio announced that I would be starred in a college musical entitled *Campus in the Clouds*, and I was really on top of cloud nine. On my way at last! But I was tumbled off the cloud the day the Japanese bombed Pearl Harbor, and World War II began. The picture was shelved, and I found myself twiddling my thumbs, waiting for the next break. I started dramatic lessons with a famous British coach named Flossie Friedman. The first time she heard me read, she stared at me as though I were a visitor from Mars, and she said, "Oh, darling! You must be kidding with that accent. I'm afraid we shall never be able to kill it!" Right she was. I still have that strong Texas tone and inflection, and I think I'll die with it. But Flossie tried, and she did help, a little.

Family affairs were getting complicated, too. Tom was in junior high school, and he was developing into a very wise, Christian and considerate boy. Whenever there was any movie publicity work going on around the house he just disappeared, quietly and completely. He knew that the deception I was practicing in passing him off as my brother was hard for me to bear and to continue. He told me again that he could never lie as I was lying, even for his own mother. He couldn't, he said, because he was a Christian, and Christians don't lie. That stung me, but my ambition was strong enough to smother the lie and the guilt, and I told myself that I was doing it for him, for his future. I loved him; I was proud of his natural musical ability, of his peace and serenity.

I was beginning to be acutely aware of a deep void and emptiness in my life; nothing satisfied, nothing gave me any sense of security. I began to read books on peace of mind, eastern philosophy and mysticism, looking for an escape

43

hatch from a life that I knew was wrong. Talk about inner chaos!

I attended church every Sunday with my husband, his parents and Tom, but I didn't let it do very much for me or to me. I left my faith on the church steps after the service until the next Sunday. I kidded myself into thinking that God would understand why I couldn't go all the way with Him, and that some day, when I was really safe and secure and ready to retire with enough money, *then* I would give more time to Him and His work. (Get the money first, Dale; God can't blame you for wanting *that!*)

The minister of the church (First Baptist, in Hollywood) was Dr. Harold Proppe. He was an upsetter. He preached sermons that probed my heart. It seemed to me that he was throwing spiritual shoes at me and saying, "If they fit, put them on!" They did fit, sometimes so tightly that my toes ached. The old defenses would rise up in my heart and mind, and I would go away in a resentful pout, and the next Sunday morning I would find some excuse—any excuse—to stay home.

One Sunday he took a crack at those people who had God-given talents in music, and who refused to honor God's house by using them there, for God. I was furious; I just *knew* he had aimed that remark straight at me. I thought to myself, "Brother, if you only knew how demanding show business is, you wouldn't say that. I'm lucky to be here once a week!" Tom read my mind. After the service he looked at

44

me in a searching, knowing way—and I knew that my son really had my number.

We were so busy, my husband and I, that we saw less and less of each other. At the studio I worked like a slave to get that four hundred dollars a week, and I did a lot of shows for the boys in the army camps; my husband went with me as often as he could, playing piano for my songs, and doing a lot of spot jobs necessary for his acceptance into the musician's union. That's the way it is in Hollywood. Schedules aren't arranged for the convenience of man and wife and children; you go where you have to go and do what you have to do, and married bliss can wait. We were making money, but . . .

All of a sudden Joe Rivkin went into the army and I was left on my own. It was a bad time for that to happen (my contract was up for renewal), and inasmuch as I had had only two small bit parts in pictures, I began to worry about it. Sure enough, one day I learned via the studio grapevine that the contract would not be renewed. In a fine frenzy I phoned Joe and told him that I was fed up with pictures and that I was going back to radio. Did he know of an agent who might help me in radio? He suggested a man named Art Rush.

Three days later, following an audition, Art took me to NBC for a tryout on "The Chase and Sanborn Hour," starring Edgar Bergen. I got it. I worked harder than hard, and things seemed to be OK until I turned down the invitation of a top executive to have dinner with him in New York. Such an invitation is usually accepted by the unwary beginner. I told him that I had a previous engagement with an old friend in the music publishing business—and the exec turned cold as ice.

I never meant to insult him, but he took it as a personal affront and days later he informed me that I would "never get anywhere in this business running around with musicians and music pluggers." He gave me another chance and another invitation to "lunch," but again I was unable to accept it. That did it. The following fall I found myself replaced after the fourth show with no hope of getting another commercially sponsored program for that season. (I tell this not to pat myself on the back for refusing to compromise my talent, but simply to say that I had too much pride in accomplishment to buy my way. I did not want to become obligated to anyone, in any way, to further my career. I had promised myself that I would never get trapped in such an involvement. I have always been infuriated with men who used their high position to acquire the scalps of hapless and heedless women. This was one area where I stuck to my guns, and I have never regretted it.)

Just as I received my notice of release from the Chase and Sanborn program, Art Rush took off for New York; he had a date with his number one client, a fast-rising, singing cowboy named Roy Rogers. I had seen Roy only once, at Edwards Air Base, where he was appearing in a camp show with the Sons of the Pioneers. (I had done an audition with them in Chicago, two years earlier.) He seemed like a very nice guy—and certainly well liked by young and old.

I liked Art Rush both as an agent and as a person. I liked him a lot the day he told me that he had gone to Bethany College in West Virginia to prepare for the ministry, but halfway through he decided that he was not called for that and changed his course. That didn't dampen his faith or destroy the effects of an early Christian training in his home and his church. All through college and all through his later work in recording studios and on the radio networks, he never lost his love of God and the Bible. He talked a great deal about the Bible, and of how he was trying to apply its laws to his life and work. This impressed me deeply, and though I left him in a fit of irritation to go with another agent, we parted friends and I was really sorry to leave him.

(Agents take a beating, sometimes, but they are not as bad as they are painted. Looking back at the agents I have known, I think of them with real respect, and even affection. I think God must have had a hand in sending three of them—Joe Rivkin, Art Rush and Danny Winkler—my way. They gave me very sound advice about my career and my personal life, and I am forever grateful for that. Joe Rivkin said to me many, many times, "Work hard, go to bed early, keep yourself in good shape and don't get mixed up in your private life." How right he was! Art's inclination toward the spiritual life was a stabilizer I sorely needed. Danny Winkler guided me with a steady hand to a contract with Republic Studios which was to mean much in my later life. God bless them all —all three!)

Actually, it was Roy Rogers who was responsible for my breakup with Art Rush. While I loved to discuss religion with Art, I just plain got fed up with his talk about that cowboy. He'd get going on Roy at the drop of a hat, and I resented it. Here I was because of the collapse of the Chase and Sanborn job, with my whole career in jeopardy, and here *he* was taking off for New York to gab with a star who already had it made! In no uncertain words I informed Mr. Rush that I'd had enough; inasmuch as he didn't seem to have time for both me and that cowboy, he could just take care of Roy Rogers and I'd take care of myself. I left him and signed with Danny Winkler, who got me a year's contract with Republic Studios. I started a picture for Republic two weeks later. It was a country musical called *Swing Your Partner*, with Lulu Belle and Scotty (of the "National Barn Dance" show) and Vera Vague from the "Bob Hope Show."

I must have been doing something right at Republic. They picked up my option at the end of the year and subsequently cast me in nine more pictures. I worked so hard that I met myself coming and going. ("Work hard, go to bed early. . . .") Near the end of the first year I took time off for a tour of the army and air bases in Texas, and with my accompanist, I worked myself into insensibility every twenty-four hours. I enjoyed it, and I think we brought a little sunshine into those soldier hearts. But today, I still flush with regret when I think of the opportunities I had to say or sing one line of spiritual hope for those boys. Since I had no spiritual awareness at the time, I couldn't share it with anyone else.

Things were going along beautifully when Herbert J. Yates, the boss at Republic, called me up to the front office. He had just returned from New York, where he had seen the musical hit *Oklahoma,* and he was planning to produce a new kind of western with the *Oklahoma* treatment. I gasped when he told me that the picture would star—who else?—*Roy Rogers!* I hesitated, mumbling something about my ambition to get into a big sophisticated musical, and that I had never thought of myself doing Westerns. Still, my heart reminded me, I had loved Westerns ever since I was a kid in Texas —had *always* loved cowpokes and horses, as a good Texan should—but my whole theatrical ambition had been on the musical comedy side. I wasn't sure.

Mr. Yates *was* sure. I was a singer, *wasn't* I? I had a definitely western (Texas) personality, *didn't* I? And, being a Texan, I could ride a horse, *couldn't* I? (I didn't tell him that I hadn't been on a horse since I was seven years old!) I just kept my mouth shut about *that,* and I did the picture. It was called *The Cowboy and the Senorita.* Art Rush's pet, Roy Rogers, was the cowboy, and I was a Mexican girl named Isabel Martinez. Joe Kane, the director, said I sounded like "Si, si, you-all!"

The first day on location was a riot—half fun and half plain misery. When I got ready to ride, I didn't even know which side of the horse to get on, and I had to be shown how to hold the reins. Roy Rogers looked at me in amazement, and his eyebrows climbed a few notches. He said, "I thought you could ride."

I said, "Well, it's been a long time since Texas."

On that set almost immediately, I *liked* Roy Rogers, in spite of all that had gone before. He was no phony Hollywood character; he was honestly down to earth, as comfortable to have around as an old shoe. He had dared to be himself, and his star was rising rapidly. I enjoyed working with him.

It wasn't easy. One day I had to come riding at a canter down a steep slope. How I stayed on that horse, I'll never know! I bounced around so hard that the temporary caps on my teeth flew off. What was worse, the horse *stepped* on them! I had the time of my life stopping the horse, and when I did Roy came ambling over to me and drawled, "Well, I never saw so much sky between a woman and a horse in all my born days." He then *allowed* that I should take some riding lessons—if I wanted to stay alive. I knew he was right; he knew a lot about riding. He sits a horse like he is glued to the saddle. I tell him that it's his Choctaw Indian blood that accounts for it, but it's probably because he learned to ride the simple but best way— bareback—on his boyhood farm in Ohio. To this day, I get a thrill every time he rides out into a rodeo arena.

Between shots on location Roy and I talked a lot. Slowly but surely he got into my heart. He told me one day about a writer on a movie magazine who asked him why he had adopted a little orphaned girl as his first child, and he told me what he had told the interviewer. He had been visiting and entertaining in an orphanage in Louisville, Kentucky, with Pat Brady and the Sons of the Pioneers. A little girl there "got hold of me and just wouldn't let me go." From the minute she saw him, this little tot, with her dark hair and deep blue eyes, grabbed hold of his pant's leg and hung on. She followed him all over the place, tugging at him until he picked her up. When he had to leave she burst into tears and held out her arms to him. For months afterward, he couldn't get her out of his mind.

Some time later he was appearing with the Sons of the Pioneers at the Centennial in Dallas. (I was appearing there at the same time, but we never saw each other!) He asked a friend, Bob O'Donnell, where he might find a little girl to adopt. Roy and his wife had just about given up hope of having a baby of their own after three years of marriage. Bob O'Donnell told him about Hope Cottage, an orphanage full of adoptable babies.

Roy told the rest of it almost wistfully, with a low-voiced intensity that reached my heart: "My wife and her mother and I came back to Dallas a few months later and we went out to look over the babies. When we had looked at a few, I stopped by a bed, looked down and saw my little girl! I knew instantly she was the one for us. We named her Cheryl Darlene, and she is really something."

Kids! He loved kids. I think that was the first real spark that flashed between us, the first bond of common interest. All my life I had wanted kids, a lot of kids. As a child in Uvalde, Texas, I used to sit on the bank of the Nueces River and dream that some day I would marry Tom Mix and have six children. Every Saturday afternoon in Osceola, Arkansas, I watched old Tom and his horse and all but worshipped them. As it turned out, I came pretty close to my dream, didn't I?

He also impressed me with his lack of egotism. He never thought he could act; he didn't even think of himself as any great shakes as a singer —and he was really good at that. From the first, I felt that he had a great native talent that somebody ought to discover, and give him the break he deserved. Roy was always himself, on the screen or off; he was "The King of the Cowboys" to a tremendous audience, and that audience loved him. He was also the boy next door, a breath of clean country air, a handsome, two-fisted man sitting easy in his saddle. And he was always interested in children—particularly sick and handicapped children. My eyes would fill up when I would see him climb down from the saddle to put his hand on the head of some little crippled kid. There was no show about it; he meant it. Like everybody else who worked with him, I fell under his spell. This one was no

Hollywood ham; he wore no movie facade. I liked that—and I liked the man.

I was sitting on a particularly frisky (and downright mean) horse one day on location, dressed to the teeth in city clothes and wearing high heels. Roy had warned me to watch the horse, and to watch those heels—if they ever got caught in a stirrup as I was getting aboard or getting off, I could be dragged to death. I listened, but it didn't register too well. I was thinking of other things as I sat up there listening to the wonderful Gabby Hayes read some funny offstage dialogue and twisting that wrinkled old face of his in contortions that made me roar with laughter. In my amusement, I threw my head and my body backwards, and the horse thought it was a signal to go. He bolted; I slipped from the saddle (on which I was sitting sideways); one of my heels caught in the stirrup, and I grabbed the saddlehorn hanging on for dear life. Gabby yelled, "Grab her, Roy!" Roy reached me on Trigger just as I was losing my grip on the saddlehorn and picked me up like you would pick up a sack of potatoes. Hero saves heroine! I could have been killed. I more than liked him, right then.

In those days I was an extrovert on the outside and an insecure introvert on the inside. I was as uncertain about my work and my future as Roy was, but we both kept quiet about it. He helped me to hide it with his irrepressible good humor; he could drawl a wisecrack in the face of disaster. We were doing a "two-shot" one day, standing close to each other. The producer had told me, "Always show your best face," which meant showing it at a three-quarter angle. It turned my face from Roy and jabbered away at a tree a hundred yards behind him! The producer shouted, "For the love of Mike! You're supposed to be talking to each other, not to some tree a mile away!" Roy said, "When she looks at me, I'll look at her." It almost broke up the party—and it fixed me good. From then on the public got my straight profile—good or bad.

Like I said, Roy's blunt and honest—and *helpful*. He went out of his way to help me in everything I did, and heaven knows I needed help right then. He showed me how to "take the action," in riding a horse, in my knees and forelegs, and how to lean back when I was pulling my horse to a stop. That was really helpful, for while he had Trigger, a wonderful and well-trained horse to ride, I drew horses with the disposition of a convict breaking out of jail. I always seemed to get what the cowhands call cold-jawed critters—horses who always have to be held on a tight rein. That's one of the reasons why today I seldom show my upper arms in a formal gown: my biceps developed like a professional wrestler's, and no pounding or massaging has been able to knock them down! It was easy enough for Roy with Trigger; he was a natural there, but with me it was strictly a case of blood, sweat and tears. After thirty-odd films with him, I can hold my own with a horse. I'm no Annie Oakley, but I can get by. Roy compliments me, now and then, with something like, "Well, at least you don't look like a sack of meal in the saddle!" I hate to think what I might have looked like in those first films if it hadn't been for him.

We were a studio family: Roy, Gabby Hayes, Pat Brady, the Sons of the Pioneers and me. We spent most of our waking hours together. We saw the best and the worst in each other. Roy was the acknowledged head of the family, and I felt as easy with him as I did with anyone of my own flesh and blood. Little did I dream that one day in real life he *would* be the head of my family! Still, much as I liked him and the studio people, I kept telling myself that a woman could go just so far in Westerns, and that it was always the handsome cowboy who held the spotlight, never the leading lady. I still longed for a non-Western musical—and a Broadway show.

Our first picture was an instant success and I was immediately cast with Roy in another one. The exhibitors said, "They're a good team; don't change it." Before I knew it, I had filmed eight more Westerns, and I began to see that I was being typed as a Western player. I asked to be cast in some other type of picture where I could star and not be just a part of a team, but Mr. Yates turned a cold shoulder. He said that I would be suspended if I refused to go along with the Westerns. Expenses were heavy, and I couldn't afford suspension, so I decided to stay in the saddle until Danny Winkler (my agent at the time) could spring me into a different kind of film or into a radio show. He did manage to get me on the Jimmy Durante radio show, and on another one with Jack Carson, the comedian.

I struggled—and hard—to improve my performance in every picture. After the shooting was over for the day, I would look at the rushes of the film shot the day before, studying every gesture, movement and expression, looking for mistakes and bad spots that could be improved. I still had a tendency to cheat a little in getting my three-quarter angle in scenes when my face showed, and if that face didn't look just right in the rushes, I'd worry myself sick all the way home. Then I'd go to sleep thinking about it instead of saying my prayers. I could hardly wait for the next day's shooting, when I could redeem myself. My ego grew to be as big as the Empire State Building. It was a monster. It is a monster to many in show business— and I pity them! This madness for personal success unbalances the whole of one's life, if one gives it free rein. It was doing that to me; I couldn't see it then, but now I know that I was sacrificing the most precious things in life —love, marriage, children—to satisfy that unrelenting drive to establish myself. It is one of the most pernicious of sins.

Let me say here and now that show business, in itself, is not sinful. To me it is a wonderful profession, in that it brings joy and often emotional release to those participating in it and to those who watch the finished product—the show. Just as the Bible says of money: it isn't the money itself that is bad but the inordinate, consuming love of it that is sinful. So it is with show business! It is the lust to get to the top, the passion to get to where the money is that is bad—evil. It is the exclusion of all the really good and decent values of life in the effort to get your hands on the prize that destroys so many of us.

Yes, there are a lot of people in show business who are caught—burned and consumed in this flame of greed—and there are a lot of others who are *not!* There are good ones and bad ones in every line of work—even in the Christian ministry. As Roy says, "When you send for a plumber you don't always get a good one."

As my career progressed, my marriage declined. My husband was a fine, talented man; he was the first man to encourage and help me in the entertainment business, and I shall forever be grateful to him for that. But due to the demands of his profession, he was also a night person who worked with dance bands while the rest of the world was asleep. He worked in the late afternoons and the evenings, and his social life came afterward, usually in the small hours of the morning. My work hours were exactly the opposite to his. I was often up at 4:30 A.M., worked until 7 or 8 P.M., and fell into bed after dinner in complete exhaustion. We had no life together. He scored films for Republic; I rushed here and there giving performances for the USO and the Hollywood Victory Committee in addition to my work at the studio. Perhaps, if I had quit making pictures and made a home, it would have worked out, but neither of us thought of giving up our precious jobs. It was the fault of neither of us and of both of us *and* of the relentless system to which we sold ourselves. It was Hollywood —and a typical Hollywood tragedy. In 1945 we were divorced.

I had lost another husband, but I still had Tom, and my conscience began to talk to me about him. Because of the scant time I had at home, I was giving Tom as little attention as I had given my husband and to my sorrow I knew it. I tried harder to find time to have talks with him when I got home from work, and I began to discover things in him that I had missed for too long. He had developed into a fine Christian —thanks not to me but to the training he got from my mother and my good mother-in-law, who had left us now. They did what I should have been doing through the teen years of his life. I could see a concern for me in his face, and I vowed by all that was high and holy that "when I had it made" I would be the kind of mother he deserved. But not just yet, Tom.

Roy was married to Arlene Wilkins, a very pretty girl, quiet and reserved, and a good partner. They had two children—the adopted daughter, Cheryl, and Linda Lou, their own natural daughter. Cheryl could have doubled for Shirley Temple, with her honey-colored hair and bright brown eyes. She was definitely an extrovert; she was the pet of the set, and she knew no strangers. She had been photographed almost as much as little Shirley, for the movie magazines were forever publicizing Roy and his family. She had an avid interest in everybody, and, as a true Texan, she could talk the ears off a billy goat—just like me! I used to look at her and think, "She's so much like me; she could easily have been my child."

Linda was different. She was shy—a pretty little girl with blonde hair and huge, sparkling eyes which did most of the talking for her. She was on the quiet side, like Roy and her mother. She spent a lot of time with her maternal grandparents, and she got very little publicity, and wanted less. They were a lovely family.

Roy talked a lot about them in the gab sessions between shots on the set. One day we got to talking about religion. I declared my faith in God and in Jesus Christ as the Saviour of the world, but I quickly compromised that by saying that I was not what you might call a 100 percent Christian, since I met God only at church services on Sunday. Roy sat listening, and saying nothing until I asked him if he believed in Christ, and if he was taking his little girls to church and Sunday school. His answer really cut me down.

"No," he said, "Sunday is my day to relax. Saturday nights we usually play cards with friends, and we sleep late Sunday mornings. But aside from that, I'm not completely sold on all this business about God and Christianity. I've played a lot of children's hospitals and orphanages, all over this country, and what I've seen makes me wonder why a helpless, innocent child should be born with a bad heart, or with cancer, or with crippled legs when he hasn't done anything wrong. Why does God let that happen? Maybe His eye is on the sparrows, like the Book says, but sometimes I think it isn't on those poor kids. If you can explain how God can let innocent children suffer, I'll change my mind about going to church."

He hit me with that, and it hurt—but he had more. "When I was growing up in Ohio, I used to listen to the traveling evangelists who came to our little church in Duck Run. They would preach up a storm and then a lot of town characters would go down front and get saved. In a week's time they would be back where they had always been. I didn't see any difference in them. Then another preacher would come, and these same guys would do it all over again. I don't buy that."

Wow! I just sat and stared at him. Since I had gone down the church aisle twice—once to accept Christ and again to join the church—and since that hadn't seemed to make much difference in my life, I kept my mouth shut. I didn't, yet, have the answers for all that.

The Pioneers knew I had a son, and of course Roy knew it. But the publicity department at Republic and the front office didn't know it. One day Dorothy Blair, who was on the publicity staff, came rushing out on the set with the look of a hunted animal, took me aside and whispered hoarsely in my ear, "Dale, do you have a son?" A columnist had just called, saying that the army induction center had reported that a recruit named Tom Fox had named Dale Evans as his mother. In relief I admitted it and explained to her how the deception had been set up during my first screen test. She said, "Just keep quiet." When another member of the publicity staff asked her about it she gave him a blank stare and said it was nothing but a ridiculous rumor with no foundation whatever. I wished at the time that it had all come out in the open, for I was weary of the deceit, but it didn't come out. Tom went off to play in an army band, and I went back to work—sadder, and no wiser.

Right out of the blue Danny Winkler had a call from RKO about a western musical they were planning, and they wanted me for the ingenue lead. It was called *Show Business Out West*, starring Eddie Cantor and Joan Davis. I was beside myself with joy; this was the break into musical comedy, *at last!* It came at a good time. Republic had refused to give me a promised salary jump, so I left that studio and sat down to wait for the RKO musical. I also left the Roy Rogers' shows, since I couldn't do them and the musical, too. We regretfully said good-by, and I waited—and waited. The picture never got off the ground, and I was left high and dry. Something or someone should have told me then that I was never meant for the musical comedy stage, but they didn't. I was about ready to quit when Republic called and asked me to come back on a very good contract. I muttered and mumbled, and went back to the saddle again.

Roy and Arlene were looking forward to the birth of another child, and Roy was sure it was going to be a boy. It was—Roy, Jr., or, as we knew him later, Dusty. Dusty was born by Caesarian section, and eight days later, a blood clot formed. The doctors were helpless, and Arlene died.

This was *real* sorrow; my troubles seemed insignificant every time I looked at Roy's stricken face.

The months that followed were terrible for him and for his children. How would he ever take care of them? He was working unbelievably long hours at Republic, and the minute he finished a picture he was off on personal appearance tours to make the extra money for publicity, wardrobe—and the family. His salary was brutally small, considering the fact that he was number one at the box office; his fan mail was astronomical, and he even had to pay the bills involved in answering it with no help at all from the studio. With all that, he had little time to think about running a home. Arlene had always done that, and here he was with the family on his back. He had a series of nurses and housekeepers and companions for the children, but it was rough going even with that help. Six months later he bought a ranch near Lancaster, California, called Sky Haven, up near the top of a mountain. Nearby was beautiful Lake Hughes.

He drove me up there one Sunday, and it was quite a ride. The mountain road wound and twisted up steep grades with no guardrails; all the way up, there were only two places where you could pull out to pass another car. My heart was in my mouth, and I almost asked him to turn around and take me home. But we made the top—and it was worth the trip. There were flowering almond trees around the small rustic ranch house, ducks swimming on the lake, and there was Cheryl and Linda and Dusty, who welcomed Daddy with a joy that hurt me in my heart. It was perfect. Being with Roy up there, I felt completely at home, and I realized that we had a rapport born of years of struggle in our work together. We were somewhat opposites in temperament, but that was all to the good; it gave us good balance with each other. He said that he felt easy with me; we seemed to know exactly where we stood with each other.

As time wore on our attraction for one another deepened. Neither of us wanted to rush into marriage; we wanted to be sure it would *work*. Roy had his family; marriage meant that I would become a part of that family, and I knew something of the problems a stepmother faced. Roy had never made any profession of Christian faith, and I had no really personal relationship to Christ; there was no real help from religious faith for either of us. I kept wondering about his children. Could I adjust to them, and would they, could they, adjust to me? Could I discipline them? I remembered my own resentment at correction, as a child, and I remembered how I resented the correction of my own son by others, when he was a child. Problems, problems, problems.

Tom had solved his part of the problem by getting engaged to Barbara Miller, a fine Christian girl. He had changed his course. Instead of pursuing the musical career I had planned for him in symphony work, he had decided to become a teacher of music in order to help children to a career—and to God. It was a stunning blow to a mother who planned not wisely but too much, but how grateful I am to-day for his decision!

Roy helped again. We were sitting on our horses in the chutes of a rodeo at the Chicago Stadium late that fall of 1947, waiting to be announced, when Roy asked me, "What are you doing New Year's Eve?"

I had no plans for New Year's Eve—which was months away!

"Well, then, why don't we get married?"

And, what do you think I said to that?

You're right. That's exactly what I said.

4

Two old friends, Bill and Alice Likins, asked us if we wouldn't like to be married in their beautiful home on the Flying L Ranch, near Oklahoma City, and we accepted the invitation almost before it was out of their mouths. This was good; it would save us from the usual spectacle atmosphere that always prevailed when movie stars had a wedding in Los Angeles. We wanted a quiet wedding, with as little publicity as possible. Art Rush (who was still Roy's agent and manager) and his lovely wife would be the only attendants, and Bill Likins would give me away.

We did get one piece of publicity, even though we thought we were keeping it all a secret. On a radio broadcast, Louella Parsons broke the news that we were to be married, and where—and she also told the world that I had a grown son. I was frightened at first, then relieved beyond words that the long deception about Tom was over at last. Tom and Roy liked it, too. These two had come to respect and admire each other deeply. Roy was impressed with the way Tom had conducted himself, with his musical ambition, his practical Christianity and his love of little children.

Thank you, Louella: you solved a real problem for me, and I'll never forget it!

New Year's Eve came—with increasingly dismaying gusts of sleet and snow. The wedding was planned for 5 P.M., and by four o'clock most of the guests had made it to the ranch, with congratulations for us and something less than congratulatory remarks about the storms they had struggled through. My mother, my father and my aunts arrived from Texas. Tom and Barbara and Barbara's sister were the last to arrive, after a real ordeal with the snow—*and* a leaky radiator—from Los Angeles.

So the guests were all there, and we could get going. Then we discovered that Bill Alexander, a close friend and pastor of First Christian Church in Oklahoma City, hadn't put in an appearance. No minister, no wedding! Bill was nearly *two hours* late. The storm was bad around Oklahoma City, and he had the worst fight of all of us to get through to the Flying L. We were so glad to see him, when he blew in through the front door, that we didn't notice his old frontier clothes. With frock coat and string tie, he was decked out as he thought a marrying parson on the old frontier should be garbed. We didn't even notice it, until the ceremony was about to begin!

Roy was as nervous as a kitten up a tree. I laughed at him. These men! I laughed too soon.

As I was dressing for the ceremony, a strong chill of foreboding rushed over me. I suppose most brides go through the same experience, but I wasn't thinking of most brides that day— only of me. I'd been married before, and it hadn't worked. Was I sure this time? I was alone in the room, all by myself, with no one to help me, no shoulder to cry on. For the first time in my life, I knew how much I needed *God!* I ran into an empty clothes closet, shut the door and just stood there, my heart pounding like mad. It was as though I were standing on a mountain top, before an awesome, questioning God. I felt weak and inadequate—and I *knew* I couldn't go through with this marriage without His help. Haltingly, I prayed.

"Dear God, you know who I am and what I am and what I have been. You know what a great responsibility I am taking on marrying this man with three motherless children. You know the problems that will come. Please help me. Help me with the courage and the understanding to establish a Christian home for these children—the kind of home You gave me. If You don't, I'll never make it."

I didn't hear any bells, or have any blue-lighted vision as I said, "Amen," but a deep, re-assuring, strengthening calm welled up in my heart. It was like the floodgates of a dam opening to set free the deep waters in which I had floundered for so long. I stepped back into the room, finished my dressing, and heard the strains of "Here Comes the Bride" from downstairs.

Bill Likins gave me his arm, and we walked into the big den and took our places before the huge fireplace. Bill Alexander was there, all set to start the ritual; Mary Jo Rush, my matron of honor, came up beside me, and we stood silently waiting for Roy and Art Rush, his best man. We waited five long, long minutes—and no Art, no Roy! I almost ran for the nearest exit. Finally they came, almost running into the room, looking a little disheveled and out of breath. I looked daggers at Roy; he just stood there and rolled his eyes toward heaven. I swear, I hardly heard Bill Alexander read the ceremony. When it was over, Roy kissed me and Art Rush exploded, "What a way to start a wedding—with the house on fire!"

It seemed that someone had thrown a smouldering cigarette into a trash basket, igniting the paper in the basket and the curtains hanging above. As Art and Roy passed the door of the room, they saw the flames, dashed in and put them out, and rushed on downstairs for the ceremony.

The storm had become a blizzard as the reception line formed; we had to send for the state troopers to help the guests find the motels in which they were to spend the night. It was wild, but nobody complained—least of all the two principals of the wedding.

It took two days to clear. The second night of our honeymoon, Roy suggested that it was a nice clear night for coon hunting. I looked out of the window at patches of snow still on the ground, and I almost said, "Man, you've got to be kidding"—but I didn't. The minister had said "for better or for worse," and while this was definitely worse, the better was that Roy had just promised to attend church with me the next Sunday, so—I went on the hunt.

Have you ever gone coon hunting? It's something. You tramp around in the cold dark following the hounds; every once in a while they let out a yelp, as though they were hot after the coon—just to keep you interested. You stumble over rocks and stumps and holes in the ground, with only a flashlight to help you—unless you're lucky and the moon is out. It wasn't out that night. Along about midnight the men reckoned that the dogs were lost (I knew we were!) and that we should build a fire and wait for them to show up. We drank gallons of hot coffee and waited, and waited. Finally Roy suggested that he might take me and the other women home, while the other men waited for the dogs. I stumbled through the dark to the car, muttering to myself, "What have I done? I'm no sportswoman. I should have married a college professor." But when we got back safely home, I repented those words—a little. I made up my mind to try to like hunting and the out-of-doors, to please my man.

We went out again another night, and this time the dogs did better; they treed two coons in a big oak, and Roy called me to come and see them shake the coons down. There were seven dogs yelping and jumping at the base of the tree and our flashlights picked up four eyes glittering in the branches. The men shook the tree vigorously, and down came the coons, into the most sickening fight I have ever seen. I let loose a barrage of protest and accusation that made the men stare at me in open-mouthed disbelief. Roy was quiet for a moment, then took my arm and walked me away from the scene. "Maw," he said, "I'm afraid you'll never be a hunter. You'd better not come any more."

That was all right with me. Two coons against seven dogs didn't look like a fair fight to me, and I was fed up and fighting mad about the whole business. Roy explained patiently that the coons were actually faster and more savage than the dogs, and if the dogs didn't get their prey they wouldn't try on the next hunt, and coons were *very* destructive creatures, and . . . It went in one ear and out the other. I'd had it—for keeps!

Back in California, we looked for a home. Roy's children were still living at Lake Hughes, and Tom was at my little house in North Hollywood, attending classes at USC. We found one up at the top of Vine Street, on the side of a mountain, built there by the late Noah Beery. It was a beauty—a large two-story Spanish home with a glorious winding stairway, the largest master bedroom I have ever seen, and with a wrought-iron balcony overhanging the driveway. The grounds were beautifully terraced and dotted with huge trees. There was a big basement: this would be our den.

We moved in. I'll never forget that day. Furniture and "fixin's" poured in from Roy's house and mine, plus Marion (our housekeeper) and Virginia (our nurse), and a pack of hunting dogs who were parked in a huge pen Roy had started building the day after he bought the place. We opened barrel after barrel, argued where to put this furniture, this silver, this glass, until we could do no more. I cooked a huge pot of spaghetti for supper. What a day! What a home!

But it took more than moving in to make it a home. I knew that, and planned for it. When we had announced our engagement, the studio had said that the public would not be interested in a married couple doing westerns, so I would have to devote my time to running the home while Roy got himself a new leading lady. This was quite an adjustment for me—and for the children, who naturally resented me in the role of mother.

One day while I was arranging the furniture in the living room, little Linda Lou stopped me with this remark: "That isn't your furniture. It's my Mommy's!" I started to rebuke her, held my tongue for a second or two, and then said, as gently as I could, "Honey, your Mommy has gone to heaven, and she doesn't need this furniture any more. So now you and Daddy and I will have to use it." She turned and walked away without a word. I knew this would happen. Roy was working long hours, and I was alone with the children—as *step*mother. I was on the defensive—edgy, and a little frightened. It would have gotten worse if Tom had not walked in one day to suggest that I start taking them to Sunday school and church—that God could help me do what I was unable to do for myself. I thought it over, carefully. The next Sunday I attended the evening service with Tom.

Tom denies it, but I will always believe that he conspired with Dr. Jack MacArthur on the sermon that night. His sermon topic, "The House That Is Built on the Rock," didn't mean very much to me until he began to explain that *any* house built on the rock of faith in Jesus Christ *could and would* survive anything that came up against it—illness, death, poverty, suspicion, greed, selfishness, deceit, lies—you name it! It was as though he had known I was coming to church that night, as though he were throwing his rocks right at me. They hit me square in the middle. I twisted and dodged and squirmed under the barrage, but there was no escaping it; I sat there looking into my heart and hearing it shout "Guilty, guilty, *guilty!*"

When he finished the sermon and extended an invitation to the congregation to accept Christ as Saviour, the invitation had my name on it, and I knew it. I felt a pull from that altar, but— no, not yet. I still fought it off. Tom read the story in my eyes and he said, "Why don't you go? Why not make it right with the Lord now? Give Him your life, and let Him give you the peace I've watched you struggling for—for so long?"

I was defensive with him: "Tom, I *am* a Christian. I've been a Christian since I was ten years old. Isn't that enough?"

"No," said Tom. "You don't really know Christ. I've watched you reading all those 'Peace of Mind' books, and all that 'Eastern philosophy' stuff, and it hasn't helped you one little bit. If you really knew Him, all you would need would be your Bible and your faith in Him. *You won't find peace until you understand that.*"

I *wanted* to go down that aisle, but I just didn't have the courage. There were voices whispering to me, "All these people will know you're a no-good sinner, if you do that. They'll talk about it, and it will be all over Hollywood in twenty-four hours. . . . Don't rush into this thing; think it over for a week or so." Voices! My mouth opened for me to say to Tom, "Give me until next Sunday; I want to think." (What a stall! I'd been thinking about it for nigh onto twenty years!) Tom's eyes were filled with tears and pity. He turned away, without a word.

Roy was away on a trip, so he couldn't help me. I felt miserable and alone, as I drove home, ran upstairs to my bedroom, dropped to my knees beside the bed and cried as I had never cried in all my life. The dam broke, and it all poured out in a long, broken, stammering confession. When I had cried myself out, I started to pray quietly in a spirit of repentance. Never before had I talked with God in such a spirit, but I did now. My whole past stood up before my eyes, revealing all the lost years like an un-rolling carpet. I shuddered at what I saw—sin, sin, sin—and all because I had refused to know and follow Christ. I had held Him only like an ace up my sleeve against the possibility of future punishment. I cried out in agony, "God, Lord God, forgive me! Just let me live until next Sunday, and I'll go down that aisle and make it a public confession."

He let me live. When the invitation was given the next Sunday evening, I bounced out of my pew and fairly flew down the aisle, grasped Dr. MacArthur's hand and was ushered into a small prayer room for prayer and consultation with a counsellor. I came clean with God, not audibly shouting my misdeeds but remembering them before Him, asking Him to come into my heart and wash me clean by virtue of the blood He had shed for me on Calvary, to create a new clean heart and a right spirit within me, to break me if He had to but—please!—to take my life and use it for His glory.

An indescribable peace washed over my heart, washed out the dirt there, washed me clean and into a totally new creature. As I got up from my knees, I felt as though a crushing burden had fallen from my back and shoulders, and I felt as free as though I were walking on clouds with my feet not even touching the earth. I looked around me as I walked out of the church. The sky was brighter, the grass was greener, the flowers were bursting with a color I had never seen before. Every tree, every weed along the highway sang and waved to me. How great it was to be alive and free. How great Thou art!

Now I knew the meaning of the words of the Book: "If the Son therefore shall make you free, you shall be free indeed" (John 8:36).

Roy was home when I got there. I said to him, "Honey, I've just made the greatest decision of my life; I have dedicated my heart and my life to Jesus Christ." I was ecstatic, wild with joy. He looked at me with those penetrating, thoughtful eyes of his, and he said slowly, "I'm glad for you, Mama, if it makes you happy—and it sure seem to be doing something like that, right now. But be careful, won't you? Please don't go . . . overboard."

I suppose I might have been mad at that, or hurt, but I wasn't. That day, in my new frame of mind, I couldn't get mad at anybody or anything. Besides, I knew what he meant. He was thinking the same thing that my mother had been thinking when she said, "Dale rushes into things. . . ." Roy always looks before he jumps; he didn't want me to jump too far, too quickly, too impulsively.

Let me explain this business of going overboard for Christ. The more I look over my whole great spiritual experience, the more I am convinced that the newcomer to Christ *has* to go overboard for Him. That had been my trouble: I had always wanted to stay in my selfish little boat; but once the vision of Christ came clear, I was like Peter—I wanted to go overboard—wanted to go the limit in faith.

What does it mean to go overboard, anyway?

Not long ago I gave my personal testimony at a meeting held at the San Fernando Music Center to introduce an organization called Space Age Evangelism. This group is trying to create a religion-oriented park here in California —a public attraction reproducing the scenes of the Bible in a Holy Land setting. It will be informative, exciting, educational, faith-inspiring—and altogether beautiful. The enthusiasm of the group in this effort to bring the Bible alive to the visitors at this park is something to behold. They know their subject; they have done their home work—their research in the Bible. They are vibrant, concerned Christians who are willing to go out on a limb with this project, as a means of communicating God's boundless love to an unbelieving, heedless world. And sure as shooting, there will be those who will say they have gone overboard. They will have a lot of wisecracks and derogatory remarks about the project and the people backing it: "It's just another money-making scheme. . . . They're a lot of religious fanatics." But— *why?*

Why can't we think big about God? If we feel called by Him to be used in a big, unusual undertaking, if we want to go overboard in a new way, what's wrong with it? The enemies of God don't mind going overboard in their schemes to defeat Him. Peter went *really* overboard once, when he left his boat to walk on water toward Christ, and it was only when he took his eyes off his Lord and began to be afraid that he began to sink. So it is with

76

our faith! When we pay more attention to others than we do to our Christ, when we care more about what people will say and less about what God will say—then *we* begin to sink, in losing our witness. When the Holy Spirit fell upon the followers of Jesus at Pentecost, they went overboard with a vengeance— and they didn't care what the unbelievers said about them. They were accused of being drunk —and early in the morning, at that! Did they care? They did *not*. Some of the more timid ones may have backed off in the fact of this slander, but most of them defied their slanderers. Certainly Peter did that; he won souls that day. He had a new power to save souls because He had seen his resurrected Lord and felt the surging power of the Holy Ghost within himself, and he *had* to transmit that power to others. He just couldn't help going overboard. He knew whom he had believed, and he was ready to lay down his life for his Master. *This* time he kept his eyes on Jesus, and he did *not* sink back into apathy and fear. It can happen to us today, if we are willing to get out of the boat and if we want to see big things happen for a big God.

No, I don't mind folks saying I have gone overboard for Christ. He has done tremendous things for me; He has revealed great truth to me, and I will not let anyone laugh or threaten me into silence about that. I think it's time that more Christians went overboard, got up and stepped out of their pitifully small denominational and cultural boats and got their feet wet in the great wide surging sea of struggling, suffering humanity. If we have experienced His love and forgiveness in our lives, if we have found healing in Him, if the Spirit has fallen upon us and empowered us, then let's speak up for Him; let's get going for Him. It isn't something we *might* do; it is an obligation.

I guarantee this: if you will keep your eyes on Him, He will never let you sink. Many, many mornings I wake up with thoughts of God, or how He is working in my life. I lie there and think, "I must write this down; I must pass it on to someone else before I lose it." But, often I negelect to write it down, and so I do lose it, and, losing it, lose another chance to witness. Paul said, "*Now* is the accepted time of salvation." We don't have yesterday and we don't have tomorrow; we have only the now. Speak— lest you forget!

Often, too, when I start thinking about my early failures in marriage, I want to go overboard more than ever in sheer gratitude to God for changing all that past error and guilt into present-sense joy. I was searching for the security of real love in those misadventures, and it never occurred to me to look to God for the only perfect love that exists for any of us. In my emotional and spiritual immaturity, I was looking for that Dream Prince to ride up in shining armor and sweep me away to endless love and contentment. I never quite realized that I was no prize lily, myself! I have a lot of compassion for those who are looking for perfection in others, jumping from one romance and marriage to another like so many restless, overdiscriminating bees jumping from flower to flower, always tasting and never satisfied. I was like that. Not until I let go and let God take over my life and my love did I find satisfaction for the deep needs of my soul. There is no water to really slake the thirst of a questing heart except the Water of Life which is found in Jesus Christ, who is the Way, the Truth, and the Life. When we drink deeply of this Water we are satisfied beyond measure; we thirst no more; we are content where we are, *and we can offer the Water to those around us. We must offer it.*

If this is going overboard, then I'm overboard. I'm a good piece from the boat—and I love it with every fibre of my being.

But I remembered Roy's word of caution: "Please don't go overboard." He said it in the spirit of love, and I accepted it in love. He also said that day, "And don't start pushing me to make the same decision you have just made. Maybe I will, but if I do, *I want it to be my own decision.*" I promised. But promise or no promise, everything seemed to work toward that moment of decision for him. He began to notice a change in me; the Christian life I was leading now was something new, and it was contagious. Example is always better than nagging, when one is near the gates of the Kingdom. I started taking the children regularly to church and Sunday school, reading the Bible at dinner and hearing their prayers at bedtime. The seeds were falling.

One day Frances Eilers came to see me. She was the wife of Leonard Eilers, the cowboy

evangelist. She had met my son, Tom, at a youth
meeting some years before at their ranch, and
she and Tom had made a pact to pray me into
the Kingdom of God. She gave me some things
to read, among them a Bible in which she had
written on the inside cover verses 10 to 31 of
Proverbs. I sat there with her and read it, and
the heavens opened. I was humbled, head to
heels, by what I read. I asked her to have lunch
with me at the Brown Derby, and in that play-
ground of movie stars and show people she told
me more about the Power of Christ than I had
ever dreamed of before. God works in mysteri-
ous places His wonders to perform. She has been
a lovely influence in my life ever since; so has
Velma Spencer, the wife of Tim Spencer, one of
the Sons of the Pioneers. Velma made me a
member of a sorority called Lambda Theta Chi
(Life Through Christ). That sorority for married
women has helped me beyond words.

I never went to church without asking Roy
to go along. When he declined, I made no issue
of it. One Saturday night we had a huge party
in our big den. It was a roaring roomful of show
people who couldn't imagine any party without
drinks and cigarettes. It got to me, and I said
something to a friend about why I no longer
cared about cocktail parties and why I no longer
smoked or drank; that now I was interested not
in whooping it up but in fulfilling my respon-
sibilities to three small children. Roy misunder-
stood it, and we had a real to-do about it; it was
one of the few arguments of our marriage, and

it was a good one. I retreated to the bedroom in tears.

The next morning (Sunday) neither of us mentioned the incident, but when church time came I didn't have a chance to ask Roy to go with us. He announced that he was going with us. The party had broken up early in the morning, and during the sermon I noticed that Roy's eyes were closed. I thought to myself, "A lot of good this sermon will do him; he's sound asleep." To my amazement, when the sermon was over and the invitation was given, he sat up straight, squeezed my hand and said, "Maw, I'm going down there." And go he did. He had made his own decision with no pressure from me, and I was never happier in my life. He was baptized, with Cheryl, that same Easter Sunday night. There was now a spiritual bond between us that has never broken.

Not long after this, Danny Winkler (my agent) called to ask if I would like to do the leading role in the London company of the musical *Annie Get Your Gun*. A year or so earlier, I would have jumped at it; this was the big time toward which I had been shooting all my life. But not *now*. A little late, that offer! It was clear to me now that I would work with Roy if I worked at all. So it came about that Art Rush and I decided that we would buy back my contract from Danny Winkler. (It cost Art and me $2500 apiece, and it was several years before Roy knew that!) This meant Art would be agent for both of us. I felt a little foolish about it, since I had left Art so long ago because of his attachment to Roy Rogers.

Two more things happened that year that made us sing for joy. Tom and Barbara were married at Fountain Avenue Baptist Church, with Linda and Cheryl as junior bridesmaids. Most of our family came from Texas and Arkansas, and I wept a bucket of tears at the sight of Tom and Barbara standing there side by side. It was a marriage made in heaven; both were committed Christians. How grateful I was that Tom was not "unequally yoked" with a non-Christian! If I had handpicked a wife for my son, I could never have done better than Barbara Miller. God had blessed me in letting me see this marriage.

And in December I learned that I was to have a child. I accepted it as a miracle. My doctor had told me during a medical examination before obtaining a marriage license that it would be impossible for me to bear another child without extensive surgery. God, and not the doctors, always has the last word! When the gynecologist told me over the phone that a baby was on the way, I laughed long and loud. "Laugh or not," he said, "you're pregnant." He was right.

The second month of my pregnancy I came down with German measles. I didn't know what that meant, or that it spelled danger for my baby. I was given a shot of gamma globulin. Twice after that I had to take to my bed to prevent a miscarriage. I wanted this baby desperately; in my secret heart I wanted a girl this time, but I made up my mind to be content with either girl or boy—just so long as it was healthy.

During this time people would ask me, "Can you tell us something really *tangible* that the Lord has done for you since your conversion?" I never resented it; these folks were from Missouri, and they only wanted to be shown. And I had one good answer for them. Our church had a radio ministry every Sunday afternoon, with hymns and a dramatization of actual conversion experiences. Of course I was glad to go on the air for them. Up to the time of my conversion, I had always suffered acute attacks of stage fright when I performed before the public. When I felt "the fright" coming on the first time I sang and spoke on this church broadcast I stopped and prayed that God would work through me, that I would feel within myself that He was speaking and singing through me as His agent. The sense of relaxation and freedom that came over me is indescribable; I felt no fear, no nervousness whatever. In the modern idiom, "the heat was off me," and I breezed through it without a tremor or a tremble. We had little time to rehearse on that program, and some of the roles I played were far more difficult than anything I had done before. I was amazed at what came out of me when I listened to the rebroadcasts.

About the end of the second month of my pregnancy, I developed a severe case of laryngitis. I was hardly able to speak above a whisper. The slightest vocal effort would plunge me into hoarseness; but I sayed on the broadcasts, certain that God would help me through—some-how. I would go to the studio armed with cough drops, lemon and honey—and sounding like Louie Armstrong! When it came time for me to step up to the mike and sing or speak, I would bow my head and ask God please to "clear my vocal chords enough for me to do this broadcast for Your glory"—and believe it or not, my voice would come over clear as a bell for the entire taping. When it was over, I had no voice; I was whispering again. That happened every Sunday afternoon during my pregnancy!

Would you call that "something tangible"?

When I was five months pregnant and Roy was away one day filming a picture, a brush fire broke out in the hills behind our house. You've seen newspaper pictures of those California brush fires, and they frightened you. They really are terrifying. The Cass County Boys (a group I had once worked with in Dallas and who were now working with Gene Autry) were there, re-hearsing with me for a TV short, and Roy's father was there. We called the fire department. The fire came closer and closer, and the men in the house used all the garden hose we had try-ing to stave off the flames. The fire raged on be-yond their streams of water in a high wind and through dry grass, until the flames were within six feet of the house. Dusty was taking his after-noon nap. I stood beside him with my unborn baby writhing within me, praying, wondering what to salvage, thankful that the other children were in school.

I prayed so hard for the fire department to

come that my nails dug into the palms of my hands—but it never came. I was about ready to run for it when the wind shifted and the fire turned off in another direction. My doctor came to give me a sedative; Roy raced one hundred miles home to help, and he knew what I meant when I said that God had heard and helped me before he got there. Don't tell me that the day of miracles has passed!

At seven months the doctor took a blood count and gravely informed me that I had Rh-negative type blood factor and since Roy had the positive factor, our baby might have difficulties. My blood count had slipped dangerously; I was prone to anemia.

At 8 P.M. on August 25th, I knew my time had come. Roy drove me to Hollywood Presbyterian Hospital. Art Rush came to keep Roy company through what we all thought would be a very long night. But shortly after midnight Robin Elizabeth arrived. Groggy and weak, I turned my eyes to the glass-enclosed oxygen box and saw a pretty, delicate little girl kicking her legs. My first question was, "Is she all right?" To which someone answered, "She looks OK." I smiled as they wheeled me out past Roy, Art and my mother. Roy kissed me and said, "Honey, she's beautiful; she has little ears just like yours!"

Roy rode as grand marshall of the Sheriff's Rodeo the next day; he announced the arrival of Robin Elizabeth to ninety-odd thousand people in the stands. I was beside myself with happiness, laughing and resting in a roomful of flowers. Dr. Jack MacArthur dropped in on the third day and gave me a book to read. It was the strange story of John and Betty Stamm, two missionaries who had just been killed by Chinese Communists, leaving a six-month-old baby girl who was carried to the China Inland Mission by a Chinese Christian woman. I thought Dr. MacArthur gave me a rather grave smile as he left, and I was uneasy for awhile.

The next day a nurse was giving me a bath. I complained that they didn't bring my baby to me as often as they brought other babies to their mothers, and that when they did bring her she was sleeping so soundly that I could hardly wake her up. Robin was pretty, all right—but I told that nurse that once while I was holding her up to the light, she looked faintly oriental. The nurse avoided my eyes, cleared her throat and asked, "Are they going to let you take her home?" She tried hard to be matter-of-fact about it, but it made me more uneasy than ever.

"Of course I'm taking her home. Is there any reason why I shouldn't?"

She looked at me and she said, "Tell your doctor to tell you the truth about her."

My heart began to pound; I demanded that *she* tell me if there was anything wrong, but of course there were restrictions which forbade her doing that.

I called my doctor and told him that he had better come to the hospital and tell me if there was anything wrong with my baby. He came, and he told me as gently as he could. Robin was not responding to certain routine tests; they couldn't tell how she would progress, but she had been in an oxygen tent ever since her birth, and that wasn't too good. He suggested that we take her home and love her and enjoy her, "Because, in cases like this, love does things that nothing else can do." My heart turned to cold stone. I was too numb to cry. I prayed, "Lord, I know you understand this. I don't, but I trust You."

Unbidden, the scene of yesteryear in the corridor of a Louisville, Kentucky, hospital flooded my mind. That was the day when I promised God that if He would save Tom from infantile paralysis, I would put my life in His hands. I flushed with remorse, and promised God that I would not question His wisdom in allowing Robin to come to us in this condition—that whatever He willed I would accept. I had already dedicated her to the Lord, and I felt that she would be used in some way to glorify Him, since it was miraculous that I could have her at all.

The pediatrician who was taking care of her told us that he suspected she was Mongoloid. He explained the characteristics of the Mongoloid child: the square little hands full of creases, the tiny ears, the undeveloped bridge of the nose, the slanting eyes. When he came to the description of the eyes I told him indignantly that she had Indian blood on the daddy's side of the family, and that would account for the slant in the eyes. I rationalized the whole prognosis and refused to accept their indictment of our baby.

We were advised to place her in an institution as quickly as possible, before we became too attached to her, because she needed special care which we couldn't give her at home. We refused to do that. We felt that God had sent her to us for a purpose, and we would never find that purpose if we were to put her away. Roy said, "We'll just take her home and love her and raise her as best we can, and trust God for the rest." Someone else said, "Of course, these children hardly ever live long, and that is a blessing." That was meant well, but it went into my heart like a knife. Putting my baby away was unthinkable.

The night Robin and I were brought home from the hospital, after she was tucked in her crib by her nurse and I was safely in bed, I heard her singing, the way babies often do just before they go to sleep. I thought, "How could anything be wrong with a little angel like that?" But in my heart I knew. I turned off the bed lamp and lay in the darkness, crying my heart out. In exhaustion, I finally fell asleep. Sometime around midnight I woke up with a start. There was a definite Presence in the room, so pronounced that I felt I could almost reach out and touch it. It was warm and bright, comforting, bringing peace to my heart. It was clear to me that the Holy Spirit of my loving God was there to calm and strengthen me for what was ahead. I breathed a "Thank You, Lord. I know it is You. I'll be all right now," and went back to sleep until I heard Robin cry at about 6:30 in the morning. For a long time I never told a soul about this experience; they would not understand; they would think I had been out of my mind. But it was real—*very* real.

Two months later I left for New York to do a TV show with Gabby Hayes. When the Super Chief reached Chicago and we had to change trains, I searched the magazine counter for something to read, something to give me a lift. The current *Reader's Digest* had an article by Pearl Buck—"My Child Stopped Growing," and there was a book by Dr. Norman Vincent Peale, entitled *A Guide to Confident Living*. I bought them, and got on the train. The Pearl Buck article rang a bell of hope for my Robin; it described her so perfectly I started to cry, then I opened Dr. Peal's book to the chapter entitled "How to Meet Sorrow." I devoured it—and it devoured my heartbreak. I promised myself that some day I would meet this man of God who had steadied me and given me courage and made me realize that God would meet every need as every need presented itself. I am still grateful to Norman Vincent Peale.

It was decided, after we returned to California, that Robin would be better off in the San Fernando Valley; Los Angeles and Hollywood were damp and smoggy, and the Valley air was invigorating. Until we found the place in the Valley we wanted, Robin was to live in the home of her nurse. We were busy taping a radio show for the Quaker Oats Company at that time; one night when I reached home after a hard day's work, I discovered that Robin and the nurse had moved out, lock, stock and barrel.

They thought it would be easier for me if she was moved when I wasn't home. I walked into the deserted nursery and let out a bawl like a cow just deprived of her calf. I waited two days before going out to see her. I found her in a lovely sunny room and in a home of serenity and love—and I was glad.

Robin was difficult to feed, like most Mongoloid children; her tongue was thick, and she had trouble holding food in her mouth. We had to get a special bottle and nipple for her. She was controlling her eyes a little better now, but she still had difficulty holding her head up. These babies are helpless for a long, long time, in comparison with normal babies.

I would look at her and my heart would cry, "What shall we ever tell the press and the magazine interviewers when they want to photograph our baby?" How could we shield her from a curious world? Then an inner voice would say to me, "Trust Me, Trust Me!" and I would become steady again in my faith in One who cares what happens to us more than any other can care.

I would ask our minister, "Why did this happen to us? Is it because of sin, or sins in our past lives, or was it something I did when I was carrying her?" He replied in deep compassion, "These things happen because of cumulative sin over many generations. The Bible says that All have sinned, and come short of the glory of God. None of us knows exactly why these things are allowed to happen—only God, and if we trust Him some day we will understand. This experience will cut away the dross and the tinsel from your life and you will know, once and for all, what is really important in life.

He was right. It was a refining experience for both Roy and me. That refining, I believe, is necessary even if it is painful, if we are to be used of God. He had many different ways of refining people; usually the crucible is fashioned of whatever we hold most dear.

In November Roy and I went on a six-weeks' tour of one-nighters with a stage show company. It was pure agony to be separated from Robin, but I know now that it was best for me to go. In the middle of the tour I received word that Robin's nurse was ill and would have to give up nursing our baby when we returned home. The Lord provided another, who took the baby to her home until we could move out to the Valley. At Christmas we had a little party for her; the whole family was there, including my mother and father. Her nurse had dressed her beautifully, and put a little bow in her hair, and she gave all of us a big smile. I took her little hands and tried to help her raise herself up, but to my dismay I watched her little face turning blue with the effort and I knew then that the doctor's prognosis of a congenital heart defect was true. She gasped for breath and broke out in perspiration. We stood there with tears in our eyes—all of us who had refused to believe that she was handicapped to that extent. It was a sad Christmas.

In February Tom's first child was born—my first natural grandchild. Melinda Christine Fox!

I was a real grandmother; I held her in my arms and thanked God.

We moved out to the Valley—to a lovely rambling Spanish-type ranch house complete with swimming pool, cattle, horses, dogs—and a garden. Roy's father and uncle had built a little private apartment for Robin—one room and a bath—since she was nervous and required privacy. She seemed to be showing some improvement, and my heart sang with fresh new hope, for I knew that with God, all things are possible. Maybe . . . after all! Cheryl, Linda and Dusty had brand new quarters of their own in the children's wing, near Robin's, and Virginia, their nurse, and Emily, our housekeeper, were next door to them. I rejoiced in this big family now gathered under one roof. I rejoiced too in Gus, our green-thumbed gardener, who grew marvelous artichokes and Kentucky Wonder string beans in our vegetable garden. We also had orange trees, plum trees, and apricot trees. That summer I put up my first jams and jellies.

There was no Baptist church in Encino. I wished there were, and I wondered about the other churches. I wanted Virginia and Emily to take the children to *some* church while Roy and I were on tour, and I wasn't sure which one. One morning I answered the phone and a kind voice said, "Dale, this is Father Smith, at St. Nicholas Episcopal Church. I'm calling to invite you and Roy to our family service next Sunday morning, at 9:45. I'm interested in you—and in that baby. I want you to know that I think you have done the right thing in bringing her home with you. God has a real purpose in this child's life; you will learn some wonderful lessons from her, and God will guide you." We went. We loved this church, and we loved its pastor, Harley Wright Smith. (Just for the record, he was the key inspiration for my book about Robin, *Angel Unaware*, and he was the first one outside the family to read the galley proofs when they came.)

We attended this church regularly, studied its Articles of Faith and the Book of Common Prayer, and had Robin dedicated and baptized there at sixteen months of age. Roy, Cheryl, Linda and I were confirmed there and joined the church.

I've sometimes been asked about that—about being first a Baptist, then an Episcopalian, then . . . something else. I am asked, "What is your church, anyway?" The question never bothers me. I just tell them the truth: "I am Baptist, Episcopalian, Methodist, Disciples of Christ, Presbyterian! I don't think of the Church as a building or as a denomination; it is a body of believers in Christ—in His birth and Person and ministry, in His Atonement, His Resurrection, His Coming Again to receive us unto Himself. Denominations are fellowships. The Church is His body, and it has many members—not all of which function in exactly the same way. Who is to say that one denomination (or function) is 100 percent right and another 100 percent wrong? God is the judge of all that. Our job is to serve wherever we are, with thankful hearts for the privilege of serving; and to love and serve a God who is a God of variety and not of monotony. As long as a church fellowship has the seal of the Cross, I am completely at home there."

For me, wherever the Christ is, in all His beauty and power, there is my church. I don't think we are going to be denied heaven if our faith is right—and I've come to believe that many people are going to be surprised at whom they will see in heaven—and whom they will *not* see. The Lamb's Book of Life isn't copied from denominational records!

That summer Tom and Barbara noticed that one of Mindy's legs seemed a trifle shorter than the other, and that it seemed to drag when she tried to crawl. I had a stab of pain in my heart as I watched the little girl and that leg. Was I to suffer *this*, too? We took her to a pediatrician, who told us that our first grandchild was minus one hip socket. Tom and Barbara seemed to have more faith than I did at that moment. They took it calmly, with such assurance that the child could and would be healed. Roy was a Shriner, and when he found that there was no orthopedic surgeon anywhere near Yreka, California (where Tom and Barbara now lived), he called the San Francisco Shrine Hospital for Crippled Children, and they accepted Mindy.

I went with them to San Francisco. With my heart pounding hard again, I watched them attach a steel brace to her shoes and slide her leg into it, forcing the leg into the hip to form its own socket. Today Mindy walks as easily and as normally as the rest of us. I saw that God had a purpose for this child, too, and I thanked Him.

The incident prompted me to search more and more to discover God's purpose for Robin, and I *really* searched. At the time we were shooting a series of half-hour Westerns with Pat Brady for NBC, and working from sunup to sundown, six days a week. I studied my Bible in my car on location more zealously than ever, and now and then a gleam of light broke through; but it was hard and exhausting. When I read in a medical magazine that there was a doctor in San Francisco who was doing things in group therapy for Mongoloid children, I left location and took the train for San Francisco. The doctor was kind—and honest. He promised nothing, but he told us to try a powdered extract from the pituitary gland of a young calf; it might improve her muscle tone, and enable her to stand on her feet. He also suggested some orthopedic therapy for her legs. Her nurse and I took turns at that amateur therapy. Today I wonder why we tried her so with all that exercise, at a time when her little heart was in such poor condition. But we tried.

Roy and I attended the meetings of a new "Hollywood Christian Group" during these days. It was started in the home of the late beloved Henrietta Mears, Director of Christian Education at the Hollywood Presbyterian Church. She was deeply interested in the spiritual welfare of the people in show business. Tim and

Velma Spencer, Jane Russell, Connie Haines, the late Porter Hall, Roy and I and several others knelt in meetings held in each other's homes and asked God to help us reach the entertainment industry for Christ. We had a different guest speaker each night, often someone in show business or in some related industry. It was, and is one of the great spiritual influences of my life.

Two movie magazines, learning of our church affiliation at St. Nicholas Church and of our interest in the Hollywood Christian Group, asked me to do a faith article on Robin. I declined, saying, "God hasn't yet shown me exactly what He is going to do about little Robin. But when the time is right, I'll give you an article." The magazine editors understood, and shelved the idea. I shall always be grateful to the press for the compassion and understanding they showed in not printing all the facts about Robin. They never did a home layout on us, without letting us edit her pictures. Although we never admitted that she was Mongoloid, they knew it, and they said nothing.

We took the baby back to the doctor in San Francisco two months later for a prearranged checkup, and this time it was really bad. He said that Robin's muscle tone was slightly better, but that her heart condition was worsening fast and that by September it would be critical. My heart was as heavy as lead all the way back to Los Angeles. Robin was upset by the trip, and suffered with violent diarrhea. In despair, I lay down beside her in the bedroom on the train, and began to pray. One of the overhead lights was on, and I noticed with a start that there was a bluish haze gathered around it that gradually filled the whole room. I threw open the door to see if it was something that had leaked in from outside. Everything was perfectly clear down the aisle of the car. All at once I knew: the Holy Spirit had come to comfort me; I felt His warmth, and was lifted up and strengthened.

Billy Graham asked Roy and me to fly to Houston to give our Christian witness at a huge rally in Rice Stadium. I declined, because it meant that I would have to fly, and I had promised myself that there would be no plane trips for me as long as Robin was alive. I just didn't want to leave her motherless. Then word came from Texas that my father had suffered a stroke, and I *had* to fly. I tossed on my bed all the night before taking off, praying, "Lord, you know I don't want to fly, to leave Robin. You don't really want me in Houston, do You?" And the Voice answered, "Who is first in your life? Robin?" I flew, stopping on my way to see my father, who seemed to be recovering. I think it was then that I really released Robin to her Heavenly Father.

When I reached Dallas, I went out to see Miss Carson, the matron of Hope Cottage, where Roy and Arlene Rogers had adopted Cheryl. Cheryl had asked me some difficult questions about her adoption, and I wanted to talk with the folks at Hope about her. My sister-in-law, Bennie Merle, was with me. Miss Carson took

97

us on a personally conducted tour to see the new crop of babies.

There were about thirty of them, from a few days old to about three months of age. As I was going from crib to crib, loving every one of them, Bennie Merle called to me from the center of the room, "If you want to adopt a baby, just come and look at this one! This is the one I would want." The baby was a two-month-old girl with enormous deep brown eyes, a shock of straight black hair and lovely olive skin. At two months, she was holding her head and shoulders up on her elbows, and her eyes followed me around the room. I was fascinated at first sight; she was the exact opposite of Robin in every way—as vigorous as a jumping bean. Miss Carson said her name was Mary, and that she was of Choctaw Indian-Scottish-Irish descent. "That's a coincidence," I said. "Roy is part Choctaw, too." She said that Mary was to go to a home where there was Indian blood. I said I hoped it would be a *good* home where she would be appreciated, and went on to the next baby. Within the hour I was on my way to see my Dad in the Waxahachie Hospital, near our old home in Italy, Texas.

Dad had had a severe stroke, but he was not paralyzed. He was a Christian, and ready to meet his Master. I had a prayer with him at the hospital and in my heart silently committed him to God. He was to lie flat on that bed for six weeks, slowly recuperate—and die within the year. When I reached Houston and Rice Stadium I had a feeling of genuine relief for both my father and my baby. I was not over-whelmed with grief at the prospect of death—I had a new faith that conquered all that.

Later that same year I had a strange dream. I was in a houseboat on the muddy Mississippi River. Robin was in a tiny boat being towed by the larger one. There was a catwalk between them. All of a sudden there was a tremendous swell and in a panic I looked back to see her little craft almost submerged. I screamed as the water receded, flew across the catwalk and opened the door of her little house. She was lying peacefully in her crib with a slight smile on her face. I cried out her name, and she opened her eyes and laughed. It troubled me.

A week later I had a call from Texas telling me that my uncle had died of a heart attack. I thought, "This must be the end of my dream. This is what it was all about." Some folks put no stock in dreams and think they have no bearing on what is to happen. They feel the same way about dreams that they feel about miracles—the day for them is gone. I don't feel that way about it. There is too much evidence the other way.

5

Robin's nurse Claudia ("Cau-Cau" to Robin) left us; she had been with the baby day and night for a year, and she was near exhaustion. Her going was a wrenching experience for all of us, for she had been completely dedicated and devoted to our child. I wondered how we could possibly get along without her. But there is, as the Bible says, a time and a season for everything, and in my heart I knew that it was time for me to accept the responsibility of caring for the child.

Robin was restless and I think lonely for Cau-Cau; she became fretful and irritable. I was feeding her one day in the kitchen when she suddenly refused to eat and pushed her milk and crackers off the table. Tired and irritated, I gently tapped the little offending hand. She started to cry and then turned off the tears, turned around in her chair and pointed to a picture of Jesus hanging on the wall behind her. It took my breath; I had no idea that she had ever noticed the picture. There was the Christ surrounded by a group of children of all races and colors—and she seemed to see something there that I had missed. Often after that she would twist and turn until she could see it.

Virginia slept in Robin's quarters that night; in the morning she reported that Robin had been restless and crying most of the night. We didn't take it too seriously, for she had had nights like this before. Cheryl, Linda and Dusty heard it too; they had been awake most of the night fighting off the swelling and fever of an attack of mumps, but we had not taken Robin near them, so it must be just another one of those nights.

The restless nights continued, however. Robin refused her food, took only her milk and cried almost constantly. And after three days her face swelled and her fever soared; *she had caught the mumps!* A pediatrician came and gave her a shot, but she got steadily worse. I called the doctor who had examined her at the time of her birth—a fine Christian physician with a great sympathy for retarded children—and he leveled with me. He said that the infection had gone to her brain; she had encephalitis, and he doubted that she would make it. Even if she did, there would be severe brain damage. I asked him, "If a miracle should happen and she should make it, would it be possible to do open heart surgery on her, and close up that congenital defect—the hole in her heart? I will spend my last penny to help her." He smiled sadly, shook his head and said, "No. Don't do it. She would never survive the anesthetic. Keep her as comfortable as you can, and go on loving her, and learn from the experience. That is what I would do, if she were my child."

It was said kindly, but it was like the signing of a death warrant.

Near midnight I was awakened by a spine-chilling howling and wailing, coming from somewhere outside. I threw on a robe and rushed outdoors to find Lana, our German Weimaranar dog and Robin's special pet, at the door of her room. I remembered the stories I had heard of dogs wailing as death approached someone they loved, but Ruth, Robin's nurse, did her best to disabuse me of that idea—it was just a myth. Robin's fever was frighteningly high and her crying wracked my heart. Ruth's explanation that this was just a pain-reflex action from the headache did little to help. I stayed and prayed while Ruth got a little rest.

At six A.M. Virginia took over; she thought Robin had just had a convulsion. They put her in cool water and brought her out of it; we took turns walking her and bathing her face and giving her the prescribed coffee enema for inward stimulation. She slipped into a semi-coma. The doctor came, looked at her and shook his head; there was nothing more he could do.

At four in the afternoon I remembered with a pang of remorse that the other children had not had lunch and I went into the kitchen to fix something for them. They were very quiet. Standing by the sink I heard the words, "I am going to take Robin." I said, "All right, Lord. As You will." When the food was on the table I went back to find Robin breathing with an ominous rasping, rattling sound in her throat. I was dimly conscious of a bird singing in the eaves of her little house. It seemed to me that Robin and I were suspended between two worlds. Lana scratched wildly at the screen door in a last desperate effort to get inside, yelping the same bark she used whenever she stood between Robin and a stranger. Ruth and Virginia sent her away. I stumbled blindly out of the door for a breath of fresh air—and to pray. I walked with Roy, my face streaming with tears, asking God to take her quickly and not let her suffer any more. Virginia came out and said quietly, "She's gone." Never have I wept as I wept then.

Tom and Barbara couldn't come, for Barbara was about to have her baby. My father was still confined to his bed, so I asked Mother not to come. My brother Hillman came in her place. We sent the children out to their grandmother's home in Van Nuys. We thought it best that they were not subjected to the ordeal of the funeral.

I could not bear to look at Robin in death. Roy stayed with her until the doctor came to sign the death certificate, and the man from the Forest Lawn Mortuary came and took her little body away. Frances and Leonard Eilers came; Frances drove me around in her car for two hours while I cried it out and talked it out. Leonard stayed with Roy.

When Frances and I came back, the little house that was Robin's was closed and dark. I could not bear to look at it. She was to be buried on her second birthday! Virginia put away her unwrapped birthday presents. Friends came, and a flood of phone calls and telegrams began.

Roy and Art made the arrangements for the services at Forest Lawn; they took Robin's little white christening dress, a blue ribbon for her hair and a photograph of her taken at the christening. On Monday evening Roy and I drove out to the airport to pick up my brother, and we stopped at Forest Lawn to see that everything was ready. Roy asked me to go in with him to look at her. I couldn't do it. I was afraid of breaking down in front of Roy and even of doing something foolish, like trying to pick her up. I could not trust myself.

When Roy came back to the car, there was a strange beauty of peace on his face. He said, "That's the hardest thing I ever did, but I'm glad I did it. I feel at peace about her now. The minute I looked at her, I knew she was with the Lord. She looks like . . . like a small-size sleeping angel." He had picked out a little child's blue casket and he said it looked very tiny among the flowers that had come from everywhere. We drove almost in silence to the airport. I was ashamed at having let him down. The last time he had been there was the day Arlene Rogers was buried. I knew how hard it was for him.

All morning, the day of the funeral, I prayed —and out of the prayers came strength to face the afternoon and the funeral. The limousine picked us up at three o'clock. I closed my eyes and prayed all along the freeway and I felt the comforting presence of the Holy Spirit. When we pulled up at the rear of the church, I asked that Robin be carried out of the other door at the close of the service so I wouldn't see the casket. What a coward I was! How much I had to learn about conquering the flesh! Roy had promised that the casket would be kept closed during the service, covered with flowers and opened only for the congregation after I was out of the room. Dr. Harley Wright Smith, who had baptized Robin, opened the service with a prayer; Dr. Jack MacArthur delivered a short talk; Leonard Eilers made the closing prayer; our favorite Gospel hymns were played by the organist and from beginning to end a Voice whispered, "Let not your heart be troubled; you believe in Me."

Somehow, the little form under the blanket of pink roses had no real connection with Robin; what lay in the little blue casket was a shell, not my baby, and I couldn't bring myself to look at it. I was taken out to the limousine when they opened the casket. One of the attendants followed me out and did his best to make me go back and look at her: "She's beautiful. She looks like a big doll. You will never be sorry if you will only just look at her. Please! It will make you feel better." I still refused. How many, many times I was to regret that!

That night I realized that life goes on, however deep and searing the sorrow may be. I learned that there was a rehearsal with the Sons of the Pioneers, scheduled long ago and urgently necessary, since they had to leave the next morning for New York and Madison Square Garden. We had been booked for this engagement for more than a year. I thought it blasphemy, but it had to be. I had to get through it somehow, and I did, racked by the worst pain I had ever known. We do what we *must* do.

My brother came to me in the kitchen after the rehearsal was over, put his arms around me and said, "Sis, I'm proud of you. You're a real trouper. Where on earth did you get the strength to do it?" I knew that I hadn't gotten that strength from anything on earth; it was Someone in heaven who was holding me up.

Sedatives kept me quiet through the night, but I got up in the morning on the ragged edge of a nervous breakdown. I was sitting in the kitchen with Emily when the back door flew open and two strange women walked in. One of them said, "Mrs. Rogers, I know this is a bad time to come to your house right after your baby's death, but my aunt here is from the East and she simply has to meet you and your husband and see your home before she goes back."

I stared at them. This *couldn't* be! Yes, we were celebrities, but must celebrities be gawked at like three-legged calves or baubles in a jeweler's window? I wanted to throw something at them, but I'm glad I didn't. I dabbed at my eyes with a napkin and said as quietly and civilly as I could, "You are right; this is not the time to see our home, and I'm not up to showing it to you. Roy is in the den, if you want to see him." With that they shoved past me and strode into the den. I don't know what Roy said to them, and I don't dare ask. I do know that they went out of the house in too much of a hurry to say good-by.

Why do people think that show business folks are something other than human? That we are never tired, or sick, or in sorrow? I like to think that they are not inconsiderate, but that they just don't understand that we are subject to the same joys and sorrows and frustrations and problems that other people know. We live in a fishbowl, and it isn't all glamour.

I was thinking about all this the next day as I sat trying to make sense of all that had happened. Gazing up at a color etching of Robin, I recalled Roy's words: "She looks like a small-size sleeping angel"—and there flashed through my mind a verse from the thirteenth chapter of Hebrews: "Be not forgetful to entertain strangers, for thereby some have entertained angels unaware." Like the sun breaking through the clouds after many days of storm and darkness, it became clear: Robin had been a little ministering angel to our family, teaching us through her handicaps that the strength of the Lord is made perfect in weakness. She had taught us some badly needed lessons and true values in life. For two years she had been teaching us humility, patience, gratitude, too, and dependence upon God.

My hand flashed out to grab a pen and I started to write. For an hour I wrote so hard and so fast that my hand became cramped and I had to stop. Yes, I had to stop. I looked down in unbelief at the little pile of paper on the desk covered with my handwriting, and I couldn't convince myself that it was *mine*. I wanted very much to write more, more, more, but I couldn't. A curtain had fallen over my mind. I wondered.

Some days later while Roy and I were doing a radio broadcast I had a few moments to rest, away from the mike. I closed my eyes and started to pray about Robin's message and the voice came again, saying, *"Let Robin write it!* You be the instrument. You will be given her message to help others. Get yourself out of the way. Let Robin speak for herself."

The compulsion of the voice, the great wisdom of it, did not pass; it dominated me completely for weeks. Robin's story flew from my pen; my hand was moved, *guided*. I kept a tablet and a pencil handy and jotted down notes and thoughts as they came to me. If no tablet was handy, I made notes on the backs of envelopes, script sheets, the margins of newspapers. It took three months to finish it. It was Robin's book—and God's—not mine. I was merely the hand He used.

Now all that remained was to get it published.

The night we left for New York by way of Dallas, we drove past the Forest Lawn mausoleum where Robin had been laid to rest. There was an illuminated cross on top of the building. As I looked up at it, the thought of her lying there and the memory of my refusal to look at her before the funeral swept over me, and a feeling of having let her down filled my eyes with tears again. I could not trust myself to speak. When we boarded the train I couldn't even manage a thank you to Art and Mary Jo Rush, who had driven us to the station. On the train, the minute the bedroom door closed the dam broke and I was near hysteria. I wanted to be strong and to help all the others, and most of all I wanted to witness to the strength of God in time of trouble. I had denied myself the therapy of weeping, as much as I was able, and it all piled up inside of me. Now I wept for nearly an hour.

Roy said, "Maybe we'd better adopt another baby, right now."

I shook my head. "No. I just want Robin." The thought of never holding her in my arms again, of never singing her to sleep again was a weight, crushing me.

Just as we pulled into the Dallas station Roy said, "When we come back to Dallas after we've seen your dad in the hospital, I want to run out and see Mrs. Carson at Hope Cottage. I think seeing the babies might help both of us."

I hardly heard him.

Dad was much improved after his stroke, and

after a two-day visit we did drive out to Hope Cottage, just before taking the plane for New York. Halfway up the front steps of the home I remembered the little Choctaw Indian girl I had seen there two months earlier. I asked if she was still there, and a nurse said, "Yes, she's here, but she has just finished her tests and she is ready for adoption. There is a fine lady of Indian extraction here in Dallas who is interested in Mary, and she may adopt her."

The minute I saw little Mary I swept her up into my arms and hugged her fiercely. Her little arms locked themselves around my neck—or did God lock them there?

I cried out to Roy, "This is *our* child. I want her. May we have her?"

His eyes were wide with astonishment. "Are you sure?" he asked. I was sure—wildly, happily, brokenheartedly sure.

"Well," he said, "it's sure all right with me."

They promised to let us know by phone while we were in New York.

New York was hard for us this time. The press conferences were trying. I was still so emotionally upset that I couldn't make sense talking to anyone. I would pray every step of the way from our dressing rooms to the chutes, and during the show, asking God to steady me as Roy and I shook hands with the children in the stands, as we always did at the end of the show. I knew I would see Robin in the face of every little blonde, blue-eyed girl. God helped me; true to His words, He did not leave me comfortless. Each night I made it, dry-eyed, back to the hotel.

But the strain was telling on me. I got little sleep. There were nightmares in which I dreamed that I saw Robin in her casket, sitting up and looking at me with questioning eyes. I would wake up crying, trying to pray, knowing that my prayers never got higher than the ceiling. The Adversary was having a field day with me! I began to wonder if Robin was just a mistake of nature, if God really knew or cared, if her book was really His doing or simply my desire to get an affliction off my chest after hiding it from the public for two years.

There were ten days of that; on the tenth morning, hollow-eyed and shaking from shattered nerves, I said to Roy, "I'm going out in Central Park and sit there on a bench until God tells me something. I can't go on like this; I just have to have some rest and some assurance that He is directing me with Robin's book. He simply has to help me!"

I took my Bible and walked out into the lovely autumn sunshine to a stone bench near the Central Park Zoo. I bowed my head and prayed, "Thy will be done, Lord. Not my will, but Thine! But—*please* give me a word. Please give me peace about Robin and her book. Is it Your will that I seek a publisher for it? Will it help Your cause? Will it help children like Robin —and their parents? *Please*.

I looked up from that prayer and saw, walking toward me, a little Mongoloid girl about

Left: Dale Evans, Queen of
the West, age 5 months.
Right: Dale (age 5) strikes a pose
on Grandfather Wood's ranch, Uvalde, Texas.

FROM DALE'S
PERSONAL ALBUM

1940—the young staff singer at CBS during the hard days in Chicago. *Below:* Concerned about his future, but ready for it—son Tom at 5 months.

Roy and Dale — minutes after
they said "I Do!" — at their wedding in Davis,
Oklahoma, at the Flying L Ranch.

Mary Little Doe (Dodie) and
John David (Sandy) Rogers
leave the plane at Los Angeles
International Airport, after
their adoption from orphanages in Dallas, Texas, and
Covington, Kentucky. (Get the
cowboy boots on Sandy!)

The happy Rogers clan gets together for a picture at the ranch. Left to right—Roy, Linda Lou, Dusty, Sandy, Dale, Dodie; in the foreground, Debbie. *Below:* Every Sunday, come rain or shine, they worshiped at Fountain Avenue Baptist Church, in Hollywood — son Tom Fox, Roy Rogers, Jr. (Dusty), Dale, Linda Lou, Cheryl, Barbara (Mrs. Tom), and Roy.

Sandy and Dusty at Banff, Canada, during the Calgary Stampede appearance. *Below:* Little Dodie is little no more. She is 15 here, and in high school.

Eldest daughter, Cheryl Darlene, adjusts her veil for her wedding at Saint Nicholas' Episcopal Church in Encino, California.

Now, life is abundantly rich
and meaningful, in companionship with Christ.

six years old, holding the hand of a middle-aged woman whose face was cut deeply with the scars of mental anguish. The child had all the characteristics of the full Mongoloid type: the slanted eyes weak and out of control, the tiny ears and little square hands, the thick tongue, the drooling, the unsteady, labored walk. There were hundreds of office workers there in the park, walking in the noon sunshine, but I lost sight of them completely. I could see only that child walking *toward me.*

Then I saw it! I had asked God for a word, and He had sent it in this child. *He had spoken to me!* He was saying to me, "I have taken Robin so that you can speak of Me to children like this, and to mothers like this. Robin is safe in the Everlasting Arms. She is safe. Now tell others how she has blessed your life in giving you an awareness of Me, and how all the other little Mongoloids in the world can bless all these other mothers."

I fairly ran back through the park to the hotel, burst into our suite and shouted to Roy, "He did it! God did it! He *spoke* to me!" And as though God took my hand and led me, I picked up the phone and called Marble Collegiate Church and asked for an appointment with Dr. Norman Vincent Peale, the pastor at Collegiate who had written the book, *A Guide to Confident Living*, that had helped me so much. I vowed when I had read the chapter in that book on "How to Meet Sorrow" that some day I would find him and thank him. So I called Dr. Peale.

I got the answer from his secretary that I expected: Dr. Peale was a very, very busy man, working on a tight schedule; people often made appointments weeks ahead, and she rather doubted that I could see him, but she'd check and see. She checked. God opened the door for me, and fifteen minutes later I walked into his study.

"Dr. Peale, I have written a book about my baby. May I read just a little of it to you?"

"Of course; but first, we'll pray." We prayed, on our knees. I got a tight hold on my emotions, fought back the tears, and read what God had put on my pen. I looked up at him; he hadn't said a word all through the reading, and I was almost afraid that I was boring him. He looked at me with glistening eyes and said, "It's beautiful. I will help you get it published."

He sent me to his own publisher—Prentice-Hall. They declined the book because they were at that very moment launching a beautiful book written by Marie Killilea—a book called *Karen*, about a little girl who had cerebral palsy. They felt they couldn't do justice to another book of the same nature at the same time.

Then he sent me to Abingdon Press. These people were kind, but they were also wary of my "presumption that the soul of a two-year-old child should have such scope of spiritual understanding," and they doubted that "God could talk that way to a baby—or the baby to God." Two blows in a row! But somehow after that experience in Central Park I wasn't let down or discouraged.

The same afternoon I had a call from Dr. Frank S. Mead, Editor-in-Chief of the Fleming H. Revell Company. It just happened that he had been in the Abingdon office after I had left the building. He called to ask if he might read my manuscript on his way to Chicago, on a business trip. He called from Chicago and said, "We want it!"

I wept—this time in joy.

Later in the same week there was a call from Hope Cottage in Dallas. Miss Carson said, "Come and get Mary. She's yours! Could you stop and pick her up on your way home to California?" Could we! I sang, "My cup runneth over . . . He doeth all things well."

I wrote Virginia to send me Robin's little pink coat and hat. We finished our engagement at the Garden and played a few one-night engagements on the way home. The last show of the tour was in the big auditorium in Cincinnati, Ohio. Roy was idly leafing through a pile of mail on the desk in our hotel room when he came across a telegram from a woman in Covington, Kentucky, across the river from Cincinnati. She and her husband ran a welfare home for handicapped children—nineteen of them—on a farm. One of the children was her own daughter, Penny. Could she bring Penny to the show to meet Roy Rogers—*and* Trigger? Roy phoned her to bring Penny that night. He also asked her, on a sudden impulse, "You don't happen to have an adoptable little boy about five years old, do you? I mean a boy I could take home as a companion for my son, Dusty."

She allowed there was one. She'd bring him, too.

They came backstage during intermission: Mrs. Coleman, Penny and little Harry. Penny was in a wheelchair and Harry walked beside her, his hand on the arm of her chair. He was a towhead with great blue eyes just the color of Robin's. His head was too large for his body, but you should have seen that smile! He looked up at Roy, held out his hand and drawled, "Hiya, pahtnah!" We "was took" on the spot. Roy swept him up in his arms and held him tight.

Mrs. Coleman told us that he had been abandoned by his alcoholic parents and left in a terrible condition in a local motel. He had the worst case of rickets I have ever seen. He had spent eight months with his legs in braces. The doctors doubted that he would ever walk. She said he was all right mentally, but a bit slow in his reflexes. The youngsters at the home loved him; he fed the helpless ones at every meal. If we were serious about adopting him, she thought it might be arranged. We agreed to call her later in the evening.

Back in the hotel room after the performance, we talked about Harry for three hours. We wondered if we could really help him to become a normal little boy and if it would be fair to the other children to bring another "problem child" into the home after the experience with Robin. We had noticed that his walking and running were not quite free or normal.

Roy said, in a dreamy voice, "Look. Anybody

will adopt a kid who has everything going for him, but what becomes of little guys like this one? Let's take him." I agreed. I remembered how tightly Roy had held him. In the middle of the night we called Mrs. Coleman. At nine the next morning we stood before a judge, signed the papers and walked out of the courtroom with a brand new son.

Don't let anyone tell me that the age of miracles is passed. God has taken one child— and given us *two*. Usually the machinery of adoption moves painfully slowly. There is a lot of red tape and it often takes months, and sometimes a year or two; it is not often that you can take a child from one state to another, as we were doing. It took us less than twenty-four hours! The Lord giveth and the Lord taketh away; blessed be the name of the Lord.

He had given us twofold.

6

The first thing Roy did with Harry was to give him a new name: Sandy. ("All we need now is another boy to name Filthy," said Roy, "to go along with Sandy and Dusty.") The second thing he did was to take him to a Dallas bootshop and buy him a pair of cowboy boots. Sandy put the boots on laughing like a banshee. We went out to Hope Cottage to pick up Mary (she was "Dodie," now). Sandy clung to Roy's hand and my skirt, afraid we would leave him there. The fear of a child with Sandy's background is a horrible thing to see.

With Sandy in his boots and Dodie in Robin's

coat and hat, we got on the plane for Los
Angeles. Dodie took to flying like the proverbial
duck takes to water. She was as active as Sandy
was passive. She ate as though food were going
out of style. Sandy's clothes were drenched
with perspiration. I charged it to too much
excitement for such a little boy, never realizing
that he had some really important physical
problems.

Dusty had been told about the new baby
girl but not about Sandy, because we wanted
to surprise him with a new brother. We were the
last passengers off the plane; our whole family
was waiting at the bottom of the ramp and the
place was crawling with press photographers.
I saw Dusty take one quick incredulous look
at the little boy holding his Daddy's hand and
run to hide behind Virginia, his nurse. Cheryl
and Linda were enchanted with Dodie, who
took all the excitement in her stride. You'd have
thought she had spent all her life before the
cameras.

Roy got his hands on Dusty and introduced
him to his new brother. Sandy grinned and
stuck out his hand which Dusty ignored. He
wasn't shaking hands with any stranger, thank
you. And he was anything but sure about *this*
stranger. Roy joined his hand with Sandy's,
and Dusty did hold onto the strange new hand
for some more press pictures.

Sandy talked a blue streak all the way home
in the car while Dusty held his peace and his
tongue. He was still wary of this new one and
he took his time sizing him up. Dusty was six

and Sandy was five. When we reached home the two new ones were shown their quarters and prepared for bed. Dodie screamed in protest when I put her in her new crib, letting out a war whoop that must have been heard in El Paso but which died a sudden death when I gave her a bottle. Sandy took it well; he was asleep before I had finished my prayer for him.

Life began again on the home lot. Emily, Virginia and the children adjusted nicely; Sandy and Dusty were soon playing together like old pals. We had both children examined by our pediatrician, who pronounced Dodie in fine condition but who had some doubts about Sandy. We found that Sandy had practically no bridge over his nose; one side of it was almost completely closed off either from a fall or a blow from a fist. From what we had been told about his parents, we were inclined to believe it was from a fist.

The pediatrician said, "All I can say is that you've got a lot of guts, adopting a child like this."

We said, "It's OK. Let us worry about that. We'll take our chances with him."

We had the nose operated on (a new bridge built), and his tonsils and adenoids removed. We kept him at home until February, and then sent him off to school with Dusty. There were problems with Sandy. He had a hard time trying to ride a tricycle. He was afraid to climb to any high place and he had periodic spells of dizziness and vomiting. He also had enuresis, which was extremely trying for all of us. I tried everything, but he was quite unable to awaken during the night and each day fresh bed linen was required. Many times I have wept in shame over losing my temper with Sandy, especially when I remember his unfailing good humor and sweet disposition as we struggled with him. He was a lovable little boy. He and Dusty had great fun together. Conditioned by Robin to understanding handicaps, Dusty made allowances for him; he would tease him unmercifully at times, but just let anyone else try to tease him!

Thanksgiving Day I took the children out to Robin's crypt. We had talked so much about Robin that I felt it would be good for them to visit Forest Lawn. We stopped at a florist's shop and bought some beautiful bouquets of pink roses and lilies of the valley, which we placed at Robin's feet. I had been there only once—with Roy. That day wasn't too bad, but this day with the children was much more difficult than I had thought it would be. The thought of Robin in the casket behind the stone plaque burned like fire and I almost fainted. Cheryl steadied me, "Easy, Mama, easy!" and took the others off for hot dogs for lunch. I rushed home with Dodie, put her in her crib and then threw myself across my bed with one of Robin's little shoes clenched in my hand and cried most of the afternoon.

That was the last long cry. The other children demanded more and more of my attention, and I decided that they were entitled to it. Christmas came, and there was a little Christmas angel on top of the tree, representing Robin. By this time the children had adjusted to the situation even better than I had, so Robin's presence was a cheerful one, and not for tears. The wound was slowly healing.

What mental pictures I have of those days! Cheryl was becoming a young lady; Linda was attending Campbell Hall School; the boys were learning to swim and going fishing with Daddy at Malibu. Dodie would sit quietly in her crib out on the lawn watching the birds, not making a sound but following every movement. I'll never forget the first Easter we had together with the egg hunt and real live rabbits (provided by Roy) hopping across the lawn. It seemed too good to be true, after all we had been through, but it was good. For every sorrow, God provides a joy.

Dodie was prone to croup. Remembering Robin, I watched her as an old mother hen watches her one chick. There was also a record of tuberculosis in her background, and I didn't intend to let *that* get started! She became somewhat solemn with strangers—when she first met them she would make them uncomfortable by just staring at them, unsmiling, until she decided that they were all right. A big grin was the signal that they were OK.

Dusty and Sandy were a handful. I would take them in the back seat of the car when I went shopping. I also took a switch to cool off their wrestling matches. Once I really caught Dusty with a good one; he howled more in humiliation than in pain.

"Mom, I'm leaving home!"

"That's a good idea. We'll pack your suitcase as soon as we get home." Silence—for two minutes. Then, "Well, maybe I'll wait a year or two."

The two of them went out one day and picked all the rubber off the dashboard of Roy's new outboard motorboat. Roy really blew his top on this one. There was an inquisition that went on for three days and which produced no evidence whatever as to which one was the culprit. They just didn't know *anything* about it. Sandy finally admitted his guilt when Roy promised he wouldn't spank whoever did it.

Then came the day when they went up and down our street opening the mailboxes of our neighbors. I looked out of my window and saw them—and took off after them with a belt. It was a good chase, but I never got close enough to use the belt—and I never chased them again!

It was at a Hollywood Christian group meeting that we made an arrangement with Billy Graham that was to become one of the great experiences of our lives. The group was growing fast, and their activities widened. There were some spectacular life-changing conversions and wonderful weekend retreats at the Forest Home Christian Conference Grounds near San Bernardino. Tim and Velma Spencer were live-in host and hostess at HCG headquarters, a Hollywood home rented by the board. They kept the door open day and night for counselling and prayer. We had different guest speakers every Monday at meetings held in big homes with big living rooms or patios. Billy Graham came to a meeting held around the swimming pool in our backyard, and he lighted many a lamp in many a heart. Roy says, "Every time Billy comes into a room the whole place lights up." The Light is truly in this man of God.

Billy came back to visit us a day or so later and in the course of the conversation he told us that he had been invited to hold a Crusade for Christ in London. He was a bit awed at the prospect, and said that he was waiting upon God for the decision to go or not to go. I think Roy helped him go when he said, "I have a big fan club in the British Isles. We'll go over there —take Dale and Trigger and do some shows in advance of your Crusade, and then join you in London the first week you're there."

We went to England in February—the coldest month in the British year. We opened the tour in Glasgow and toured the Scottish highlands and the English countryside, driven by a most delightful cockney known as Griff. Griff was as warm as British toast. The weather was so cold, wet, snowy and miserable that I was sure the devil had planned it. We got some relief when we stopped for luncheon, dinner or tea at the country inns. Never had tea tasted so good. The coffee—well, I pass! Coffee definitely isn't their cup of tea, but the welcome we got in Glasgow warmed our hearts. The street outside the theater was packed solidly with people who shouted, "We want Roy! We want Dale! Sing us a song!" We leaned out of a window and sang a chorus or two of western songs, and they roared for more. What a people!

Edinburgh was cold, too. We stayed at the old Caledonia Hotel, just below the royal castle, and we could hear the bagpipes playing up there in the clouds above us. Never have I been so physically cold—or numb. The maid kept a fire going for us in our room, banking it at night. When I slid into bed the first night, I thought I had opened the door to the North Pole. I gritted my teeth and stretched out—until my feet touched a hot water bottle. I wish I had bought that bottle, and brought it home and given it some years of retirement in sunny California before it went where all such bottles go!

I always read my Bible before going to sleep, wherever I am, and sometimes I read a newspaper as well. I read a newspaper one night in Edinburgh to see what was happening to Billy in London. Plenty was happening. The newspaper account was full of unfriendliness toward him—critical and often sarcastic to the point of insult. They complained, "He looked like a Madison Avenue TV salesman, with his bright tie." They wrote of "little old laides singing Gospel songs," as his ship docked. They were quite dubious about "the big advertising campaign the American evangelist and his team were putting on." They doubted his sincerity— and that stung and disturbed and angered me. After all, he had been invited to come to England. There seemed to be some need for evangelism: one Sunday morning we went to an early Communion Service at the great cathedral in Carlisle and found a congregation of six.

We also sensed the pressure of opposition when we told the people of the press about our intention of giving our Christian witness during the first week of Billy's Crusade. Their eyebrows would go up and someone always asked, "What do you mean—your *witness?*" Some wanted to know why Billy had come to England when there were already plenty of churches in England. Didn't America need his preaching more than England needed it? On the whole, the press was friendly to Roy and to me, but we couldn't understand its harsh criticism of Billy.

One press lady, however, wasn't so friendly with me. When I told her that I had found the British people very kind and warm and friendly, and that we were enjoying the beautiful English countryside, she almost snarled, "Oh, don't be so trite! That's what the studios tell all you actresses to say when you come over here." I was startled at her impertinence and insulting language, but I told her bluntly that nobody had told me to say anything to anyone about England, that I spoke for myself and for no one else—and that I was not in the habit of lying. Pondering these things today, I think this underlying resentment against Americans is caused unwittingly by some of our rough riding and ill-advised visitors over there. I *loved* being there.

I prayed for Billy and I spoke for him, during our tour. How wise he was, all through those first hard days and weeks in England! He never replied to their insults. He simply ". . . set his

face like a flint . . ." (Israel 50:7), to go to
London and do what God and the outstanding
clergymen and religious leaders of England had
asked him to do. He was sincere and friendly
—and he preached up a storm every night. The
papers gradually changed their tune as the
crowds at the Crusade grew larger and larger.
What's that old saying? "Nothing succeeds like
success."

In Edinburgh we met two most interesting
people—a man and a little girl. The man was
Chief Constable William Merilees, the Queen's
personal guard in Scotland; the girl was Marion
Fleming, a tiny girl with a haunting little voice,
in an orphanage called Dunforth. She sang for
us; I can still hear it. When we left, we invited
Marion to have lunch with us at the hotel and
then we invited her to visit us the following
summer, in Hollywood. The matron at the
orphanage thought it might be arranged.

We were both sick when we reached Liverpool. As Griff drove us through the shouting,
jostling throng in the streets we were flushed
with fever and aching from head to foot, having
hardly enough strength to wave back at them.
It was the European flu. A doctor put us to bed,
stuffed us with sulfa and penicillin and started
a medicated steam inhaler going full blast in
our room. The newspaper people thought we
were faking in order to cancel a news conference
set for the afternoon, and they tried to trap us.
They stuffed a bunch of daffodils in Trigger's
mouth and had Glenn Randall, our trainer, walk
the horse upstairs to our room to present them.

When they saw our faces at the door of the room, they knew we were not faking, and the party was over.

Two days later we shuffled weakly onstage at the theater and somehow got through the performance. We had been threatened with a lawsuit if we didn't show after two days—sick or not sick. I remember clutching the curtains onstage to keep from falling.

Liverpool, Manchester, Belfast and then Dublin. Our bookers had suggested that we omit any reference to the Billy Graham Crusade— omit it there and anywhere else in Ireland. "You might get hit with vegetables." We ignored it. We don't frighten easily when witnessing is involved. We were concerned about it, yes, but our concern evaporated when we received the greatest response to our inspirational and Christian closing in Ireland that we had known anywhere—England, Scotland or even America. We got a standing ovation in Dublin. A delightful monk who was chaplain of the Abbey Players talked for a long time with us about Billy, and remarked that, "The man is doing a marvelous work." He gave us an entertainer's prayer book which was prefaced by the story of the Christian martyr Genesius, the patron saint of the Abbey Players. We liked Dublin—and the Irish.

Two days later Roy galloped Trigger out into the center of Harringay Arena in London to a deafening roar. It was as though there had never been a word of opposition to us, or to Billy Graham.

Billy preached well that day, to packed

stands. The room was packed to the rafters for the evening indoor service. I looked at Billy and wondered how he was going to get through his sermon with cameras flashing all around him. What power flowed from him that night! I could feel it mounting when Roy and I spoke briefly and sang a duet; I felt it even more after Billy's sermon. He paused a moment before giving the invitation and in that moment a man in the balcony leaped to his feet, raised a clenched fist and shouted, "Mr. Graham, why don't you pray that the President of the United States stops this war?" Billy was quiet for a split second before he replied, "Too long have we looked to man. Let us look to God!" That answer just *had* to come from God. The response to the invitation was tremendous. One of those who came forward was a well-known young British actress who had been on the verge of suicide.

Another night, I saw young men with liquor bottles in the front row, drinking in front of Billy and the choir all through the service. A man yelled, "Mr. Graham, why don't you go out to the American air base and preach to your Americans and get them to quit getting our English girls pregnant?"

But on the whole, Billy was getting better and better notices, and it was working out well. The night he closed the Crusade, there were 90,000 at Wembley Stadium standing in the rain to hear him. The Archbishop of Canterbury held the umbrella while Billy preached! I was sure when I saw that, that Billy had overcome his opposition, and I was content to start for home.

Home! Home meant Cheryl, who was attending Corvalis High School, Linda, who was attending Campbell Hall and Dusty and Sandy, who were enrolled at Northridge Military Academy—and Dodie, who had just celebrated her first birthday. I vowed I'd stay home with them from now on—and then discovered that we had a three-week tour through Ohio, Indiana, Michigan, Missouri, Tennessee and Texas. Show business! Just before going onstage at Columbus, Ohio, I was stopped by the same feeling that had come over me the day Robin died—nausea, stomach cramps and that odd feeling of being in another world and somehow apart from everything that was going on around me.

Roy was called away to the phone for a minute on a long distance call. He seemed preoccupied when he came back; when I asked him who it was, he said, "I'll tell you about it later; right now, we're on stage." Suddenly I felt release, and we went onstage.

We piled onto the bus after the show and I noticed immediately that everyone was unusually quiet. I overheard our road manager, Jack Lacey, say to Roy, "Have you told Dale anything yet?" I heard Roy answer, "Wait till we get to the hotel." In our room, he cleared his throat and started to tell me, "Dale, we've had word that . . . ."

I said, "My father is dead." He nodded.

"What time did he die?"

131

"He died just a short time before you had that sick spell, when we were going onstage." Call it telepathy, call it spiritual, call it anything you want—I have found that it is *there*—that voice between two suffering people in the great, deep moments of life.

I had to do this one on my own; Roy had to stay and finish the show in Columbus. I flew to Texas alone. My brother Hillman and his wife Bennie met me at the airfield and drove me to Italy. He must have been reading my mind during that trip, for he said, "Sis, you've got to look at Dad; he looks better in death than he has looked since he had that stroke."

I remembered Robin, and I started to beg off with the usual, "I want to remember Dad as I knew him in life," but it was a poor excuse, and I knew it. Hillman said, "Don't make that mistake again. You owe it to him and you owe it to yourself. If you don't, you'll have to go through the same agony that you went through after you refused to look at Robin. *Please. . . .*" The mention of Robin did it—that, and that awful feeling of cowardice in refusing to face up to the fact of death. Reluctantly, I went to the mortuary with my brother, his wife and my mother and saw my father.

Hillman was so right! God did a wonderful thing for me as I stood there and looked at Dad. *He removed all fear of death from me forever.* I looked and saw a Christian; I saw not a body but a soul united with Christ, and I never again allowed my human sorrow to blind me to that truth of reconciliation and redemption. And I knew that in the wisdom and the planning of God, we would all be reunited with him again in the perfect life—in the Everlasting.

Again there came unthinking fans and autograph seekers, as they had come after Robin died. A stranger from a nearby town heard that I was there, and she came with a car full of people *on the day of the funeral* to ask for autographs. My uncle was furious at their lack of respect and even ordinary decency, and he was all for telling them off, but I stopped him; most of those in the car were children. Besides, this autograph business was part of being a public figure. The mother of the children said they had literally goaded her into bringing them. They went off happy with their autographs— and I was happy for them. I was glad to have made someone else happy, while I was in the depths of sorrow. They will experience their sorrows, soon enough.

I tried to get my mother to come back to California with me for a rest—and learned another lesson. "No," she said, "not now. I have to face it alone, sooner or later, and I may as well start right now. Later, I'll come."

We cannot run from death, and its partings. We cannot run from anything. The sooner we accept the fact of death, and the sooner we resolve to work it out with the help of the Lord, the sooner we conquer it. Roy and I sometimes sing that old spiritual.

> You have to walk—that lonesome valley,
> You have to walk it by yourself—

The valley of the shadow—how we fear it, until we face it and travel it and find in it nothing of which we need to be afraid!

And there are other valleys we must travel. I went through one of the others the night Redd Harper, the singing evangelist, with his wife and adopted son came to have dinner with us. (It was shortly after my father died.) Just before dessert, the room started whirling around me, and I blacked out. Emily, our housekeeper, brought me to with the application of a cold wet towel and I dismissed it, thinking I was just overtired; but later it happened again—at the piano. This time I went to bed. The next morning I awoke with a loud buzzing in my ears, with bells ringing and the room spinning again. They got me to the hospital and the tests began. At first they said it might be a brain tumor, but later that was ruled out. It was labyrinthitis— a loss of balance due to an infection of the inner ear. For days I was so ill that I didn't care whether I lived or died. Everything inside me seemed to be out of whack: I had triple vision, my stomach would hold nothing, and my liver seemed to be bouncing around like a tennis ball. It took me two months before I could walk a straight line—and only then by pushing a straight-backed chair ahead of me.

Even after I got home, I was still deep in the valley of despondency. I thought that I had suffered just about everything, and that nobody ever had to put up with such sickness and death as I had. The very weekend that I came home, the two-year-old son of one of our friends drowned in their swimming pool—and God gave me the strength to get up and go to them and to witness to them of how He had helped me through the valley of the shadow, not once, but many times. It helped them—*and* me.

I've had more than my share of illness and death, but I have discovered this: *you can always find someone whose troubles are worse than yours.* If you have gotten through yours, you owe it to those others and to God to *go!* Go to them, and help them with your witness.

Go! Share your comfort and your faith! As we use our own experiences of suffering constructively, we find our sorrows turning to blessings for ourselves and for others. I don't argue about this. I know. I have found that it works that way.

I was to have still another lesson in this business of sharing when on a bright Sunday morning Roy and I were leaving the house for a morning service at the church. On the front porch we found an old friend who had worked in some of Roy's pictures and who had a really bad alcohol problem. Reeking of liquor, he staggered up to me and grabbed my arm, demanding, "Dale, I've got to talk to you. You've got to help me. God has helped you and given you what I need. You remember me, Dale? I knew you *when.* You've found salvation. Help me find it. *Now!*"

Roy was impatient with the intrusion, and if I ever felt less like talking to anyone with a view to helping them, it was at that moment. I was swaying on my feet, worn-out—but I couldn't

be mad with him because Jesus' words to the
man possessed by evil spirits came to me: "Go
home to thy friends, and tell them how great
things the Lord has done for thee" (Mark 5:19).
I had to stay with him.

He poured out his story—and what a story! I
gave him prayer—and a cup of black coffee—
and I took him to church! I needed the Communion Service that morning; he needed a talk
with Father Smith, the rector—so we went. I've
often wondered what the people in the church
thought when we went reeling down the aisle
to our pew, but I was too sick and distraught
to think of it then. We made it to the pew—
the weak leading the weak.

Father Smith asked him if he needed counselling—the understatement of the week! He
needed it, and he got it after the service. It was
a new start for Jack, and it lifted me, too. I
marveled at the change in our old friend. As
Stuart Hamblen says in his song, "It is no secret,
what God can do."

It was a weird performance. I suppose some
folks thought it was "out of place," but—I'd do
it again. Church was the place for Jack that
morning!

7

Mother and Roy were worried about my periodic physical breakdowns. Mother cautioned me, "You had better slow down. God doesn't expect you to kill yourself. He gave you a mind to use in taking care of yourself. Use it! If you don't learn to say no, you will be getting down to where you can't say anything."

This is one of the reasons I am writing this witness. I am unable, *humanly unable*, to go with my testimony to all the places and to all the people I'd like to reach. I know I personally cannot go to all of them, but I also know that I *must* go to as many as I can. Neither I nor anyone else knows the date of departure from this earth—only God knows that. But Jesus said, "I must work the works of him that sent me, while it is day: the night cometh, when no man can work" (John 9:4). So I work—and get as much done as I can. While it is still day for me, I shall be used of Him to the limit, wherever, whenever, however it pleases Him. Sometimes He uses us when we are in perfect health—sometimes in our physical suffering. He can have me in either.

I am constantly aware that Satan is watching and hoping that I, as a Christian, will be rendered helpless in my work of proclaiming the Good News that Christ died to save sinners. I do not underestimate the old boy for a minute. The Apostle James tells me in the Bible, "Resist the devil, and he will flee from you" (4:7). Many times in the dead of night, I awaken with a sense of foreboding or in physical pain, intuitively aware that the Adversary is at work on me. He's wasting his time. All I have to do is to tell him (although he doesn't admit it) that he has already been defeated at the Cross and that while he may some day claim my body, he will never take my spirit or my soul. Christ bought that at Calvary. I tell him that, and almost without exception, he leaves me. Satan cannot abide the name of Jesus Christ—and I intend to repeat it in his face so long as I have breath.

I found a way to say it in our little book, *Angel Unaware*. When I came home from the hospital, I found a mountain of mail from people who were reading the book. It had been published just before Easter and in a short time it was on the best seller list. God was doing everything possible to help me with *Angel*— but there was a lot I had to do for myself. I took a series of potent iron shots, to stimulate my very low hemoglobin, and went at the mountain of mail.

When I realized that this book was really going to click, I got to wondering about the royalties. (Doesn't every author think of that?) I had written the book to help little Mongolian Robins—and I came to see that my royalties, as well as my energies, should go to help handicapped and retarded children in the field of research, promotion and publicity, and to acquaint the public with this desperate need. Then I knew of no national organization specifically founded for such a purpose, and I was at a loss to know just *where* to allocate the funds. I prayed. God answered.

About a month after the release of the book, Roy and I were doing a radio broadcast at NBC when we were approached by a man and two women who wanted to take a publicity picture of us for use in a fund drive for the Exceptional Children's Foundation in Los Angeles. Exceptional Children! I liked that. I liked it even better when they explained that this foundation was a branch of the National Association for Retarded Children, headquartered in New York, which was started in 1950—the year Robin was born!

I was so overcome that I could hardly speak.

This was it! I immediately wrote the Fleming H. Revell Company to send all my royalties to the National Association for Retarded Children, and the *Angel* was on her way!

More and more now, children took first place in my life—after God. God *and* our children— that was it! God and children everywhere. One day on location near Chatsworth, in the San Fernando Valley, I saw a little boy studying me intently, especially the western clothes I was wearing. His eyes were riveted on me, and I was a little uncomfortable about it until he casually strolled over to me and asked, "Dale Evans, how old are you?" The little rascal stunned me into silence. (Roy says any woman who will tell you her age will tell you anything!) But I don't mind telling my age. I'm proud that God has given me fifty-six years in which to help Him. The boy's curiosity amused me (when I got over the initial shock).

"Oh," I said, "I'm one hundred years old."

He gave me an icy stare and replied, "No, you are not one hundred, either."

"All right. How old do you think I am?"

"You're not a day over sixty-five."

That was fifteen years ago! I'm sure he thinks, by now, that I have joined my ancestors. But I still love him for his question—and his honesty!

(Every once in a while some woman asks me if I have had my face lifted, since my age is no secret. No, I haven't had my face lifted, but God has lifted my heart and made it eternally young. I tell them that. I tell them that it is the Spirit that quickens. I have met a lot of young old people whose countenances have been kept glowing only with the light which is spiritual.)

The children under our rooftree have kept me young, too. It hasn't been a chore to take care of them, in spite of all that has happened to them and to me. It has been a most rewarding *privilege.* I remember, for instance, the trip to Hawaii on which we took Cheryl, Linda and Dodie. We had a booking in Honolulu that took a lot of time, but I have forgotten that and remembered the time we spent with *them.* Who could ever forget Hawaii, once he has see it? The fantastic trade winds rippled through our hotel rooms on the first afternoon when we sat around eating the huge fresh pineapples brought up to us; nor can we forget the tour of the island of Maui, where we swam, idling in that incomparable Hawaiian sunshine. Cheryl and Linda took hula lessons with me so we could do a song-and-dance medley in the show. What memories! And the wee grass skirt we bought for Dodie! She ran to Roy at the end of the show, jumped into his arms and sang "Jesus Loves Me." We loved the Islands, loved the people—and loved the children more than ever.

Then there was the coming of Marion, the little Scottish girl from Edinburgh whom we had invited to come over to California for a little visit. We thought when we invited her, that our family was already large enough, but . . . ! Chief Constable Merilees told us that she was "unadoptable," since both her divorced parents were still living, but that she could visit for several weeks. He cleared the way with the authorities, and she came.

A tiny, pretty, slightly bewildered girl got off the plane in Los Angeles, looking as though she hadn't expected to come this far from bonnie Scotland, and wondering where the Indians were. No Indians, but the whole Rogers tribe was there to welcome her, and her face lit up like a Christmas tree when she saw us. Larry Kent, who worked for us in promotion, was there, too; he had met Marion in Edinburgh and the plan was for her to visit them first, and then come to our home. The kids loved her at first sight, and she loved them. Dusty, as we might have expected, was wary of her at first, and Dodie sat stock-still for a long time before she accepted the little Scot. But Sandy broke into his broad grin and held out his hand in welcome, almost before she could get off the plane.

At her first dinner in our house, Marion said little and ate less. I wondered if she disliked both us and our food, and I wondered if we'd made a mistake bringing her over here. She explained it one day in an explosion that nearly knocked me flat. Staring at the table loaded with food, she said, "It isn't fair!"

"What isn't fair?"

"All this . . . all this food, and *everything*. It isn't fair that you have so much in America and that there's so little in other places. You've got too many cars, too many refrigerators and washing machines, too rich food and too much of it. In Scotland I got half of one egg on Sunday, once a week. We saved our pennies for days on end to buy an orange—and here you have them lying around under the trees on your lawn." (Never had I seen a child eat so many oranges!)

It slapped me awake to something I had missed in Scotland—and perhaps in other countries, too: I mean the *poverty*. I thanked God for sending Marion to make me aware of that— and I resolved not to miss it, the next time around.

A week before she was due to start for home, I found her crying in a corner of our breakfast room. Before I could say a word to her she sobbed, "Mama, I don't want to go home. I want to stay here with you."

"Why, child, I thought you didn't like it in America. You've acted as though you were homesick most of the time. What made you change your mind?"

"Because you are so *free* in America," she said.

That was hard for me to understand. I said that the people in Scotland had seemed quite free, to me.

"Mama, you don't understand. Over there, if your father is a plumber, you'll be a plumber. That's as high as you can go. That's all you can expect to be. But over here, you can be anything you want to be. I want to *stay*."

I explained that we couldn't keep her any longer because her visa had expired, but that didn't mean anything to *her*. She was sure we could arrange it.

We arranged. With the help of Mr. Merilees we got permission to keep her until February.

She went to school. She went to church. She went everywhere, seeing everything with her great hungry eyes—and loving it. But . . . January came, and she begged to be allowed to finish the school year before going back. She was becoming an American, inside and out. Her delightful Scottish brogue was disappearing, and we noticed more and more American slang in her conversation. (I think I preferred the brogue!) She had settled down into the routine of our home as though she had been born there, and we were apprehensive about parting with her—with tears in our eyes. We got her visa extended to June.

You guessed it: she didn't go in June either. By June she was our ward. She stayed for keeps.

She and Linda became bosom pals, playing and swimming together; Dusty and Sandy were as close as blood brothers. Dodie was the loner of the crowd—except that she had adopted the family dog as *her* property, not to be touched or abused by anyone but her. Cheryl was having her first party dress and her first boy-and-girl party at the house. Tom and Barbara occasionally brought their two little ones to add to the confusion—and the joy—and to participate in our round table discussions, prayers and Bible readings. It was heaven! And it seemed that it *must* go on forever.

Now and then there was trouble, and when there was trouble we went looking for Sandy and Dusty. Sandy had become a sort of front man for Dusty—meaning that Dusty made the spit balls and got Sandy to throw them. One day Sandy just plain swiped some of Dusty's play money and fibbed about it; I had to chase him all over the backyard before justice was served with a peach tree switch.

Another day Dusty was the crook; we found his pockets loaded with coins that we knew represented unearned wealth. Roy and I were careless about leaving change lying on our dresser and on the office desk, and Pat O'Shea had a cash box in her desk that certainly *looked* looted, so we knew where Dusty got it. We decided that a little meditation and soul-searching in solitary confinement would be good for him, and so he was locked up in the men's dressing room near the swiming pool. At noon I took him a prisoner's lunch—bread and water. He didn't object; I thought he almost smiled at me! Something was wrong here! (I discovered later that Linda and Marion had climbed up on the roof of the building and handed down tasty little snacks to the criminal below.) I let him out in the middle of the afternoon—and he still didn't tell me where he got the money. But he never forgot that time in jail—and he still talks about it!

We had help with the children. A French bachelor friend, Joe Espetalier who was custodian of the Masonic Temple in Hollywood and who guided Roy through his Masonic activities, was sort of a big brother to the boys and took them on endless excursions on those long days when we were on location or off on a guest appearance tour. And there was Pat O'Shea, our marvelous secretary, who filled in for me many a time when the youngsters needed attention and guidance. My health was in a precarious state, and Pat just took over and did what had to be done. She had a degree in psychology and she was wonderful in her dealings with people—with business associates, friends, and the whole family. In a way she is my spiritual protégé; she accepted Christ, was baptized and confirmed at St. Nicholas' Church, and I was more than thrilled to be her sponsor. She was one of the big happy family.

Roy and I were to play the Canadian Exposition in Toronto, that summer—and suddenly Cheryl decided that she wanted to go with us. We took her; her boy problem was beginning to get a bit out of hand, and we thought a change of scene might be good for her. She worked with us in the show, and she got a good share of whistles and applause from our enthusiastic audiences—so much so that she announced that she would go with us to do the show in New York's Madison Square Garden a month later. That would have meant missing almost four weeks of school at the beginning of the term, and we had to say no. She resented that. She was a teen-ager now, and she resented *all* authority. One night while we were in the middle of the New York engagement, she just packed up and went across the street to one of our neighbors, telling them that she was leaving home. The neighbors called Father Smith at the church. That was a good move, for Cheryl loved and respected him, and he could talk with her about her problem. He called us in New

York and suggested that she be sent to an excellent girl's school—one like Kemper Hall, in Kenosha, Wisconsin. We were stunned, but we agreed; she was enrolled at Kemper Hall for the rest of the school year.

I rushed out to Kenosha when we finished in New York, and we talked it all over. I made Cheryl a promise: when she was twenty-one, if she felt so inclined, we would try to find her real mother—*provided* her record at Kemper was a good one. It was better than good. She made top grades in everything and when she came home in June it was as though nothing had happened. As promised we later found her mother and Cheryl spent a weekend in her home. Cheryl is a wonderful girl, the mother of two boys and two girls.

Now I have gone out of my way to talk about this problem with Cheryl, because I know that such problems with teen-agers occur in most families sooner or later. I'd like to say a little more about this generation gap that seems to be setting so many of us on our collective ears. What it is, anyway?

A gap is just a space between two points. That's how the dictionary might put it. Our gap is supposed to be between the point of view of our young people and the point of view of middle-aged or old people. Right? It is a *generation* gap. It's nothing new. It has been around for a long, long time. We are all born as babies; we all become children; we all become adults. That's been fact for thousands of years. It didn't just pop up in the last five or ten years—or since rock music was born! As a teen-ager I used to rock and roll mightily to the tune of "St. Louis Blues"; my mother would hold her ears and say, "Do you call *that* music?" I thought she didn't understand me—that she was an old fogey. When I got to be twenty-one, I wondered how she got so smart so quick!

She understood me, all right. Because she loved me, she made it her business to understand, even though many of my words and actions hurt her deeply. She knew I was groping for something in life—sometimes in anger, striking out, stumbling, getting up and running again. She was always there to help *because she remembered how she felt as a teen-ager*. She knew a lot of things had changed since then. She had her first date when she was sixteen in a horse-drawn buggy with her older brother as chaperon. Just try to find a horse and buggy now—or a chaperon on the first date! A lot has changed: the length of dresses, hair styles, shoes, means of transportation and communication. Things change every day, but the basic human problems haven't changed a bit since my mother was a girl, or since I was sixteen. *Neither has the answer changed!* Jesus Christ is still the answer—Jesus Christ, the Way, the Truth and the Life. Jesus Christ, and He alone!

Not long ago John Lennon of the Beatles made a facetious remark, in declaring, "Christianity will go. It will vanish and shrink. We [the Beatles] are more popular than Jesus now." He said it when the Beatles were at the top of their popularity. Even then they were not happy, nor even content. They were looking for answers, and the answers evaded them. They went all the way to India to see a guru, to learn from him how to meditate and how to be happy; he didn't tell them anything they couldn't have heard at home. One by one, they were in trouble as they searched for answers—looking for them in drugs, in fancy cars and clothes, or barefooted, or in no clothes at all—and still they were not satisfied; still they did not find what they were seeking. Only Jesus Christ satisfies the deep need of the soul—only He who said, ". . . him that cometh to me, I will in no wise cast out" (John 6:37). ". . . we will come unto him and make our abode with him" (14:23). Only He!

Just the other day I read a booklet written by a brilliant American scientist. He is an expert in space physics, radio communication, radar and radio astronomy investigations, and a member of the Institute of Aeronautics and Astronautics, the American Association for the Advancement of Science, the Acoustical Society of America and the American Geophysical Union. It sounds like a page out of *Who's Who in Brains*, doesn't it? Yet, with all this, he is a man who was never satisfied (his personal life was a mess, he says) until he realized his need for a Saviour to forgive his sins and to give him assurance of everlasting life. I humbly suggest that this man is somewhat more intelligent than John Lennon. This man found the answer to the question of who made the universe, the constellations, the Milky Way, the atom—*when he found Jesus Christ.* Think that one over, you who are talking about science displacing God!

My generation doesn't have all the answers—and neither does the Now generation. But the Bible has them—the inspired word of God has *His* answers. It provides answers for the Establishment *and* for youth. (Speaking of the Establishment, let's keep it clear that the adolescent of today, the young people of today are the Establishment of tomorrow. That's why we should be sending them to the Bible *now* for the answers to the questions they're asking.)

It begins in the home—in parent-and-child relationships. The Bible says: "Children, obey your parents . . . Honour thy father and mother . . ." (Ephesians 6:12). *Then* it says, "And ye fathers, provoke not your children to wrath: but bring them up in the nurture and admonition of the Lord" (v.4). In other words, children are to love and obey their parents *for God.* Parents are to love, serve, instruct and discipline their children *for God*—as caretakers of their children for God until they are ready to move out of their own.

That was the way we did it with Cheryl, and with all the children. We did it, or tried to do it, the Christian way, and it has paid off—handsomely. Every one of those children has found Christ—and all settle *their* problems the Christian way.

Dr. Bob Pierce, of World Vision, Inc., came out to our house one night to show us some films taken in Korea, depicting the plight of little Korean orphans who were the victims of racially mixed marriages. Most of them were the children of Korean mothers and soldier fathers in the United Nations troops occupying their country. I looked around the room at our little League-of-Nations family, and I wondered if we might find room for just one more—one of these Korean orphans, maybe one about Dodie's age, who could grow up with her. No, the house wasn't big enough, but . . . We gave Dr. Pierce a picture of Dodie, and he said he'd look around and see.

We couldn't get those Korean orphans out of our minds!

8

We moved out to a 133-acre ranch in Chatsworth, near Canoga Park. There was an old brick and frame house that was large and comfortable but still not large enough; so we just built more house on each end. The children were excited about it, and no wonder. In view of what was to happen there, we should have named it Excitement Acres.

First, Dodie had a fierce attack of croup that we thought was going to kill her. She might have died if it hadn't been for a new nurse—a fine black woman named Leola. As the attack became worse and worse Dodie was actually turning blue as she fought for air. I screamed for Leola, who came paddling into the room, pushed me aside, held Dodie up by the heels, shook her, and ran her finger down her throat to release the blockage. She calmly put Dodie back in bed, turned to me and said, "What you so excited about? My old folks taught me how to help chillun like that. It ain't nuthin'." I just sat there and stared at her.

Excitement Number Two was Dodie again. We had purchased the ranch with an eye to shooting movies and TV specials there, and of renting the locations out to other companies. One of these companies came to do a "Brave Eagle" series, which was cowboy-and-Indian stuff, showing the better side of the Indians. One morning Dodie looked out of her window and saw a horde of screaming Indians come toward the house, complete with war paint and war whoops. She flew into my arms, frightened out of her wits: "Mama! Mama! Those Indians are coming after me!"

Excitement Number Three: we began missing things around the house. Naturally, we asked Sandy and Dusty about it, but we got the whole truth from the principal of Northridge Military Academy where they were attending school. It seems that the two young men had set up a trading post at the academy, selling off a lot of things they didn't think we'd miss!

Excitement Number Four: the house caught fire. We had set up a large Christmas candle on the TV cabinet; Marion sat up late that night, and went to bed without blowing it out. Along about four in the morning Cheryl's voice came over the intercom in our bedroom: "Listen, Mom. Don't get excited, but get up quick. The house is on fire." I ran down the long hall to find the living room red with the ruddy reflection of the fire. Smoke was billowing out in all directions, the television set was a blazing ruin and the piano was beginning to burn. There was a huge hole burned out in the middle of the floor. Fortunately no windows were open. We got the children out, and I raced for a phone to call the fire department. Cheryl stopped me; she had already called them. What a manager she was! While the rest of us were flying around in all directions, she calmly took the jeep down to the gate of the ranch to show the firemen the way to the house.

Dodie wailed that Bimbo, her big stuffed monkey, was in the house and Mama ran back in to get him. We stood around on the lawn in our bathrobes, and waited—in a drizzling rain. We waited a terrible half hour before they got there; I was beside myself with fear that the flames would reach the heating unit under the living room and blow the whole place to smithereens. It didn't.

When it was all over, the living room, dining room and kitchen were black, charred ruins. We set up the Christmas in the den—our first Christmas at Chatsworth.

We were filling an engagement at the Houston Fat Stock Show and Rodeo when a letter came from Dr. Bob Pierce of World Vision. Poor Bob! In all the excitement we had almost forgotten him, but he had not forgotten us. He sent us a picture of a little Korean orphan he thought might fit into our League-of-Nations home as a companion for Dodie. She was In Ai Lee, chosen from among 600 orphan "possibilities"—complete with a Dutch bob, soft brown eyes and a very, *very* solemn expression. Love at first sight! We all wanted her, and Bob Pierce went to work to clear her for our adoption. She was to arrive in June. Dodie couldn't wait.

Little In Ai Lee came off the plane at the Los Angeles airport in the arms of Bob Pierce. Roy reached for her, and she nestled into his arms without a struggle Newsmen followed us out of the airport to our car, taking pictures. Debbie (we had already re-named her!) looked at them with an uninterested expression, which never changed. With that I began to have misgivings; was she all right? Everyone tried to make her smile. No luck. She and Dodie looked each other over in sullen silence, with inscrutable eyes.

Driving down to the Goldwyn Studios (we had to report for work that afternoon) I held her on my lap and tried to talk to her. I might as well have been talking to the Boulder Dam. She could speak a few words of English (*Mama, Daddy, Milk, sleep*), but beyond that—nothing. When we reached the studio I asked one of the older girls to sit in my dressing room by Debbie while she took a nap I was sure she was worn-out enough to sleep. One of the men on the set came into the room with a big red balloon. She reached out for it, grabbed it and held it close to her face, with a grin as wide as the Mississippi River.

Debbie, dear Debbie, was home!

Home, yes, but still in a strange, new environment. At the supper table her face suddenly took on a strained, painful expression, and, not speaking Korean myself, I couldn't determine what the trouble was. I tried to question her, but not speaking English, she couldn't tell me. Betty's husband (Betty was a new nurse who had come to us when Leola left to recuperate from illness) asked her a question in *his* language (he was Filipino), and Debbie nodded in relief. He picked her up and took her into the bathroom!

I tucked her into bed that night next to Dodie, pulled the covers up around her chin, and began to teach her a little bedtime prayer. She smiled, but didn't repeat; she couldn't, yet. I turned out the light, and left them with God.

Betty reported the next morning that Debbie had fallen out of bed three times during the night; when Betty tried to put her back in bed, she crawled under it for she was used to sleeping on the floor. That went on for about six months. She was determined to sleep Korean—and to *speak* Korean, too. One day she grabbed my hand and pulled me out to the driveway where our jeep was parked. She had something important on her little mind, and she jabbered away at me in Korean, pointing at the jeep. I couldn't understand a word of it, and I told her so—in English, which she didn't understand. She put her hands on her hips, shrugged her shoul-

ders and sighed as if to say, "You dumbbell!"—
and without another word turned and walked
into the house.

That was the last word of Korean ever spoken
by that child. Within a month she was speaking
fluent English. I am still amazed at that—at the
way children learn a new language so easily
and so quickly. Perhaps it is because they have
so little to unlearn. It had made me think that
if children can pick up knowledge of a language
like that, they can also pick up a knowledge
of the love of God like that. They can accept
and build faith quickly—hold it in the grooves
of memory through childhood—and through
all their lives, for that matter. Maybe this is
what the psalmist meant when he admonished
us, "Train up a child in the way he should go:
and when he is old, he will not depart from it"
(Proverbs 22:6). Intensive training in the early
days goes deep and stays deep in the subconscious, and is held there for later need. My
mother and I can witness to that!

With all the children in tow, we went off to
do a show at the Columbus (Ohio) State Fair.
They each had a part in the show, and they
were an excited bunch of youngsters. Debbie
experienced another form of excitement. When
we got off the plane in Columbus the welcom-
ing committee and a huge crowd of fans closed
in around us, making such a racket that Debbie
almost went into hysterics. She thought it was
an air raid! She hadn't forgotten Korea, even
yet. She didn't calm down until we got to the
hotel.

The day we spent at Duck Run, where Roy had lived as a boy, was better. We saw the house Roy and his father had built, the well in the back of the house, the little schoolhouse, and we met the warm folks who lived in the holler beyond the house. It took me back to the time Roy had taken me there, just after our marriage. The tables and chairs had been moved out of the kitchen for a square dance, with Roy calling the dances. Some of the older fellows really tore up the place—and I nearly danced the shoes off my feet.

Sandy and Dusty got a bang out of Roy's ole swimmin' hole. They stared wide-eyed as he showed the boys the spot in the kitchen where he used to sit with a gun on his knees waiting for a shot at the rats that always came out at night. They hardly believed him, I think, when he told them that his mother would often tell him to go get meat for supper, and he would go out *with a slingshot* to hunt down a rabbit. I believed him. I think this is why he is such a dead shot with a gun today, even from the back of a horse.

His horse on that old farm was Babe; he rode her bareback. His father worked in a shoe factory in Portsmouth and got home only once every two weeks, which meant that Roy had to be the man of the family and do chores usually done by a grown man. He tells of plowing behind Babe and of hitting rocks and stumps that almost knocked him down. He says that one of the tests of mettle for the boys was to run barefoot over the short, hard stubble in the schoolyard without flinching. Rarely did he put on his shoes before the first frost. He finds it hard to have compassion for youngsters nowadays who feel put upon if they have to walk a block to catch a school bus. He has known the nitty-gritty of struggle for existence in his youth, and he has little sympathy for those young people of today who think the world owes them a living.

I'm with him. He believes in free enterprise— and in being enterprising. I'm with him there, too. When our children began to accept their Christmas gifts in a matter-of-fact way, as though they were something we *owed* them, he would tell them, almost in anger, of the one Christmas gift he remembered and cherished most—a Barlow pocket knife. One year he threatened to give the children nothing but a lot of pasteboard boxes so they could play with them and tear them up on Christmas Day. He told them the story of the pocket knife so often that they would put on that Here-we-go-again-kids look whenever he expressed his concern over their nonchalant attitude toward their gifts.

We had to think about other gifts, along about this time: two of our little flock left the roost. Cheryl and Marion were married. It was hard to believe that either one of them was of marriageable age—but they were—and each had decided on her one and only, so—what's a mother to do? Cheryl was married to Bill Rose on Valentine's day. She had just finished high school (which was more than I did!) and while I pleaded with her to wait a year or so—to get a little college—it was no use. She had a lovely red-and-white wedding in St. Nicholas' Church, with Dodie and Debbie as junior bridesmaids. Linda Lou was her sister's maid of honor and Marion was a bridesmaid.

Then Marion stepped off: a month later she married Dan Eaton, a Marine stationed at Camp Pendleton, California. Being Scottish (I think this was the reason) she wanted a quieter, less publicized wedding. (Cheryl had 750 at her wedding.) Marion chose to be married at home on the ranch.

So two were gone. Two from seven left five.

The weddings made me realize that the youngsters were growing up faster than I thought possible. In no time at all, they weren't youngsters any more, but teen-agers with a brand new set of interests and ideas. I looked at Linda Lou singing a song called "Seventeen," with her father. I heard the whistles of approval from the audience, and I knew she was no longer a child. Even Debbie and Dodie were growing like weeds. They sang on our shows like a couple of veterans. Debbie was the speaker and Dodie was the singer in a sister act that brought down the house. I knew they were changing, and as they grew, I began to look a little more closely at their backgrounds, to try to figure out their futures.

Dodie walked up to a wizened old Indian who was selling Indian trinkets in the street and asked him, "Are you a good Indian? I'm Indian, too, and I'm good!"

Indian! This probably started me thinking

about blood and race and color as I had never thought of them before. Dodie was Indian; Roy had Indian blood in his veins. Marion was a Scot; Debbie was a Korean. The rest of us were white Americans—but that was a distinction we never seemed to notice in our house. We were a Christian family, and that was enough. We lived and worked and played and prayed together as though we had all been born in the same house. All that race and color stuff meant nothing to us.

Folks *outside* the family seemed more interested in drawing lines of race and color between us than we did. Often, someone would marvel at our League-of-Nations family, and occasionally the question would get through to us, "How do you manage to get along so well together?" I have never resented the question. I raise it here only because I want to explain how and *why* this experiment in racial togetherness has worked out so well—and so easily— in our home.

It worked out because of the attitude we all took toward it.

Dodie was Indian. Let's start with that. I've been interested in Indians for a long, long time —especially since I met Roy Rogers! Last year I went to Denver to give my testimony at a convention of the American Indian Crusade, and it was a great experience. Just to hear those Indians sing was a thrill. They sat there together and sang together and ate and talked together as though they had always been together —Indians, whites, missionaries, businessmen, show people, folks from all over and from every church in America—folks who were interested in taking the Gospel of Jesus Christ to the first Americans. As I sang and talked and prayed with them I was ashamed of the way we have treated the Indians in this country, and I resented almost bitterly that we had called them redskins and pictured them as savages. What *is* this skin color kick we seem to enjoy, anyway? How did it ever get started, and why do we keep at it? I saw just *people* in Denver.

The Indians themselves have a quaint little story in which they explain how skin color originated. It seems that the Great Spirit decided to make human beings to inhabit the earth. He took his dough from the dust of the earth and put it in His big oven to bake. The first batch came out undercooked—pale, white (these were the pale faces). The second batch came out overdone, black (the Negroes). The third batch came out a beautiful sun-kissed tan. Just right!—The Indians!

It's not a bad way of looking at it, when you think it through. It was God who made the races, not man. And nowhere do we hear God saying that He prefers any one race to another. Again it was man who developed that superiority complex, racially speaking. When you get right down to it, it is this *human pride* of race that causes all the trouble—those of one color looking down their noses at those of another color—that's *pride,* and pride is a sin and a stench in the nostrils of God. He knew what He was doing when he created the races.

163

That's the way we look at it in our house.

Someone said to me recently, "You don't see a crow mating with a canary, do you? All nature abides by God's laws in this area except humans, and they just have to *experiment.*" In other words, the races should be kept separate and recognized as basically separate and different from each other. I'll buy some of that, but not all of it. To our home in Chatsworth Roy once brought a beautiful little yellow bird in a cage. He said, "This bird is half-canary and half-wild linnet, and it sings the prettiest song you ever heard." He was right. This bird had the lilt of the wild meadow lark and the trill of the canary. There were two birds singing in one throat, and it was beautiful. What do you mean, keep them *apart?*

Or take our dog Bowser. Bowser is half coyote; the other half is made up of chow, boxer and bulldog (we think). He has the black tongue of a chow and a coat that is a mixture of coyote, yellowish-gray and bulldog brindle. His tail curls high on his back—the mark of the chow. A more lovable dog I have yet to see. His eyes are uncomfortably human. He's as steady as a rock—not flighty and high-strung, like so many pure-bred dogs. Bullet, our German shepherd, has a fine pedigree, and so has Bobo, our black French poodle. Our pure-bred Chihuahua has a pedigree as long as your arm, and so has Smokey, our big Persian tomcat. We love all of them, but I'll have to admit that Bowser is the number one favorite with the family, *because of his wonderful qualities* and not because of any pedigree. The best of three breeds runs in his blood.

Every race has special and marvelous gifts. Why can't we look for those gifts, and learn to appreicate them? Why is it that we fear each other so? The Bible says, "He that feareth is not made perfect in love" (I John 4:18), and that "If a man saith I love God, and hateth his brother, he is a *liar*" (v.4:20). Love is not narrow, not restricted, certainly not racial! It is, as the songs says, ". . . a many splendored thing." Read Paul's definition of love in the thirteenth chapter of First Corinthians; just try to put *that* in a racial straitjacket! Jesus said that men would know us as His followers when ". . . ye have love, one to another" (John 13:35). Love is *never a* respecter of persons—nor of any particular color or race of people. The Bible calls upon us to love *even our enemies*. Is that possible? Have you ever honestly tried it? Have you ever tried to go the second mile, to bless those who curse you, to pray for those who persecute you?

We talk about these things a lot in our house —about a love that knows no fences or barriers —yes, or races.

Love does it—Christian love. Think about that love, in terms of the children in your house. Is it an unselfish love you have for them? Do we love them for their own sakes, or for our own gratification? Are we hurt and bitter when they do not return our love—when they are thoughtless and thankless? If we become angry and resentful with them, we had better take a fresh look at our motives for self-sacrifice in their behalf. According to the Bible, we are supposed to do whatever we do as though we were doing it *unto the Lord*—never looking for reward, never counting the cost, never demanding a return. I admit to shortcomings in this department with our children once in a while, but always, after I have nursed my little hurt for awhile and then have taken a good look at myself, I am ashamed. *I know I have to go on loving, come what may.*

When Jesus healed the ten lepers and only one thanked Him for it, did He stop healing? No, he continued to heal for the glory of God—and not because He expected a word of thanks.

Let love, not appreciation, be your motive, and you *win*.

Let's get back to this business of race. We were sitting around the studio one afternoon, waiting between scenes, and we fell into one of those stimulating, thought-provoking conversations that we all enjoy. One of the men remarked that he loved Joy Eilers' song, "What Color Is Love" (I sing it often, on TV), and he said it was too bad that we couldn't put the philosophy of that song into wider practice. I said I believed that we *were* making real progress in the area of racial acceptance—and another man jumped all over me saying, "I'm sick of people who go around bragging about how tolerant they are and how some of their best friends are black people. But when it comes to issues like open housing, they renege in a hurry."

There was a moment of startled silence, and then someone else said, "Oh, it's better than it used to be. The kids today don't have the prejudices we had when we were their age." I told them I believed that love was the ultimate solution. We talked about our various backgrounds and prejudices, and I said I felt that we could overcome any and all of those differences if we loved one another as we should. For one thing, we had adopted two children of different racial ancestries and these children were as much our own as our natural children. If we care for others, we love them. That follows as the night the day.

Then we delved deeper and talked about intermarriage. I said I thought it would be a pity if all the different races melted into one, and we lost all the beauties of race and color. Who wanted a sky full of nothing but one species of birds? One of the fellows said, "I disagree with you. I think we should all be one color."

Then another chimed in, "That wouldn't solve our problems; we would still be prejudiced in some other way."

I think *he* really struck at the heart of the matter. Man's *heart* must be changed—supernaturally, by God and Christ—a new Spirit must be born in him before he can truly be one. All the social and political reforms we talk so much about will come to nothing until we are bathed in the Holy Spirit of God and see each other as creatures He made in His own image—creatures He loved enough to visit in the person of Jesus Christ and whom He loved enough to provide the great sacrifice for their redemption.

What is the color of such a love? It is beyond human comprehension.

A friend told me of being at the point of death while in a diabetic coma. He spoke of the sensation of being lifted into a cloud of indescribably beautiful color: "The aurora borealis was nothing, compared to this. I heard the Voice of Pure Love say, 'Come home, Son.' That voice I can never forget."

Now we all have conditioned reflexes which affect our thinking processes and of which we are not often aware. There are subjects buried deep in the subconscious mind which may reappear in some future situation or crisis, and we can't understand it. Afterward, we scold ourselves for the way we reacted, and vow that we will conquer and change that reflex.

For instance, when one of our daughters graduated from high school she asked permission to entertain the graduating class at a mid-morning swimming party on the ranch in Chatsworth. I was delighted. Being a very resourceful girl, she, along with some of her friends, did all the inviting and preparing of refreshments. They would take care of *everything;* they wanted it that way. The morning of the party I had some shopping to do; I got back home after they were through swimming and were playing records in the den and enjoying the refreshments. I walked in blithely and made the rounds, shaking hands—when suddenly I was hit by a brilliant smile from a very dark face. Fleeting, idiotic panic rose in me as I gripped the hand of this black boy and moved on to the boy next to him, hoping he hadn't noticed my surprise. I knew I must have blushed—and I hated myself for the little scene.

You see, this is what I mean by conditioned reflex. I was of Mississippi-Texas parentage; I had spent all of my childhood in the South, and the old, familiar, deeply entrenched impressions and teachings of that childhood had surfaced in an unguarded moment. This is probably a very unscholarly way of relating it, but it's the only way I could explain it to myself afterward. I have not lived in the South for many years, but that early Southern training is still deep in my mind.

I told the man in the discussion at the studio that I tried always to be perfectly honest with myself and that with God's help I was doing my best to love and understand the Negro—and I prayed that he would try to love and understand me. I cannot help my color and he cannot help his, but we can both love the God who made us and God in turn will mold and teach us to love one another. The Bible says, "Shall the thing formed say to him that formed it, Why hast thou made me thus?" (Romans 9:20).

Whenever I visit an armed forces hospital (and I visit them as often as possible) I try never to see a disfigurement, a missing limb or eye—or a face a different color from my own. I always pray that the boy will look me straight in the eye—*for there we can communicate.* The eyes are the windows of the soul; we should understand that when we meet someone of another race. The common bond of humanity is great—forged with joy, suffering, expectation, despair. Basically, we are alike. Why can't we remember that? And each of us, of whatever color, has his contribution to make to the whole. It is a joy to me to see the entertainment world enriched more and more with the talents of different races and cultures, in every phase of entertainment. Each race has a magic of its own in the arts of expression, and they can all be justly proud—no, justly *grateful*—for their gifts and attributes. The world is beautiful because of all of them.

I feel for the ministers of the churches in this day of racial crisis and confusion; they are in one of those spots where they will be wrong in someone's view no matter what they do or what position they take. I admire those who do not flinch from doing their Christian duty as they see it, according to the Light that is in them. I feel pity for them because I know the price so many of them have paid in loneliness and isolation and even persecution, when they take an unpopular stand. Let's not be over-critical about them or toward them. Let's be prayerful and self-searching and see if we ourselves are doing all we can to further God's Kingdom and the welfare of all His children, according to the Light which is within *us*.

I cannot agree with all their aims or with all their methods; I am only wishing that those who acknowledge Christ as Lord have the same spiritual stamina to stand up and be counted for our convictions. We shall never agree on every issue but we can admit that the other fellow has a right to his opinions, and even though we differ, we do not need to hate. We are all human. As Alexander Pope said, "To err in human; to forgive, divine." Disagreements can and often do turn into hatreds; they breed fights and fatal dissensions in the Church, and I hate *that*. What would happen if every marriage broke up over every disagreement of man and wife? What would happen to the children then? And what happens to the babes in Christ when older, more experienced Christians fall out in quarrel and disagreement? What's a babe to do—and what and whom is he to believe?

Again, love is the answer—Godly, unselfish love for one's neighbor. Love is of no one color; it's made up of all colors. Since we were all created in His image and in His love, can we do less than love all His creatures?

I realize that this is an explosive subject, but the love of God has a habit of surviving all explosions, and I will rest on that. If we are guilty of racial prejudice, we are not manifesting the love of God. The Bible says that God created the world and all therein and that when it was done He saw that it was *good*, all of it, every bit of it. He didn't say, "It's all good except for the black man, or the white man, or the red man or the yellow man." No, he said it was *all* good. He created man and He left man to show some appreciation for His creation— and I humbly suggest that according to His standards, our appreciation of Him isn't anything to brag about.

Jesus said that the greatest of the Commandments was this one: "Thou shalt love the Lord thy God with all thy heart, with all thy soul and with all thy mind . . . and that the second is like unto it, . . . *and thy neighbour as thyself*" (Matthew 22:37–39). And who *is* our neighbor? Must he be one of our own crowd or set, one who believes as we believe, one of our particular race? Jesus shouts an eloquent no to that in His story of the Good Samaritan. The Levite in that parable was a Jew; the Samaritan was—Samaritan, and there was bitter enmity and hatred between Jews and the people of Samaria. Neither saw anything good in the other; but notice that the Samaritan and not the Jew is the real hero of the parable. In showing his love and mercy for one in trouble, this despised Samaritan was the Levite's neighbor. There was no prejudice in him.

All my life, I have worried about racial prejudice, and all my life I have prayed God to take it out of me. It's a hard thing to get out; it is hard to put aside *all* prejudice and to love everyone we meet with the full love of Christ. We had a speaker at one of our Hollywood Christian group meetings who asked us this, "Suppose you were on Skid Row, and a drunken old wino came up to you and asked for help. Could you put your arms around him—dirt, liquor, breath, lice and all—and sincerely say to him, 'I love you, brother, in the name of the Christ who died for all of us'?" There was an embarrassed silence, and many an eye was riveted on the floor!

What color was Jesus when He was here on earth? Who cares? The important thing about Him has never been His color but the fact that He cared enough for this many-hued humanity to identify Himself with it. We might even say that He integrated with us; but it wasn't just the kind of integration we're talking about today. He became one with us in the flesh, but He stood high, high above and beyond us in the Spirit. The Bible says, ". . . saith the Lord. For as the heavens are higher than the earth, so are my ways higher than your ways . . ." (Isaiah 55: 8, 9). It also says that God Himself is too pure to behold iniquity. We humans, *as* humans, were such an offense to Him, so unclean toward Him, that only the drastic sacrifice of His Son on the cross could cleanse us. Are you humbled by that?

I am. And I do not believe that the color of my skin, or my (supposed) Anglo-Saxon ancestry means anything whatever to God. He is interested only in the quality of the love in my heart for Him and for my fellow man. I say it again: *He made all of us and He loves all of us.*

I know that the Bible says the descendants of Ham (who are held to be Negroes by some Bible students) were condemned to serve the descendants of Shem and Japheth because Ham looked upon his father's (Noah's) nakedness, and that seems to smack of racial difference, of superiority and inferiority, of the punishment and degradation of one race and the elevation of another. But Ham's wasn't the only tribe to be punished for disobedience. Down through history, the descendants of every tribe you can think of have suffered at one time or another. Whatever our ancestry, there was a time when our forefathers were slaves! The entire Jewish nation has suffered terribly; the whips of prejudice have cut deeply into their backs, even right here in the land of the free and the home of the brave. Not only have the Jews suffered in this country—remember the Irish, the Polish, the Orientals, the Puerto Ricans!

I doubt that we can blame it all on Ham. I think we need to remember that the more powerful white man has too often and too long thought of non-white races as races created to do his hard labor! We should remember, too, that Jesus Christ came as Redeemer to save all men from the bonds of slavery and prejudice: "If the Son therefore shall make you free, ye shall be free, indeed" (John 8:36).

I find myself resenting more and more this classification by color. As a child I resented the arrogance of some of the more favored and learned people in my town calling the poorer and less learned people who lived along the river "red necks." Their poor necks were red only because, as tenants, they had to work long hours in the blistering sun. Today I resent being called Whitey just as others resent being called Niggers. In the first place, I'm not even white. I'm beige, if you know what I mean. The only folks I've ever seen who are really white are the dead ones. Our blessed Leola said once of Dodie, "Her skin is so pretty. It's like real coffee with a lot of cream, so soft and so smooth, and her eyes are sparkly pretty. I had a daughter

174

once with a skin kind o' like hers, 'ceptin it was a little darker tone. She was pretty, yes—but not as pretty as my boy Jesse. Now there's a *pretty* one. He's black, real black!" I can still hear her saying that.

Dodie watched me closely one day while I was combing her hair, and I knew something was coming. It came; she asked, "Why are you so white and why am I so tanned?" She held her little Indian-brown arm beside my white one, by way of emphasis. I reminded her that many men and women with white arms spent a lot of money and a lot of time in the sun trying to get a brown arm like hers, but that didn't satisfy her: "But you are out in the sun a lot. How come you're not as tan as me?"

I explained then that the world is God's garden and that in this garden He has many varieties of animals and plants—and people, and that it would be terribly dull in the garden if we were all exactly the same color and if we all had the same physical characteristics. She bought that.

To me, this is the best argument against wholesale intermarriage between the races. Basically I am opposed to such intermarriage, because I know that it seldom works, and that it can have a terrible effect upon the children of such a marriage. And basically I believe that each race has its own beauty and its particular value in God's creation. Would we like our pretty bouquets of many-colored flowers, if they were *all* red roses, or *all* yellow, or *all* white roses?

If one of my children should come to me and

175

tell me, "I am in love with someone of a different race; we want to get married, and we want your blessing," I think my reply would be (and I would pray God to give me the grace to say it rationally and objectively) something like this.

You know just as well as I do that you are in for trouble if you do this. People are confused about it, and there are many people who will just never accept it, or accept you, if you do it. There is a great, deep, bitter feeling against it all over the world. You will pay a high price for it—just as many other people, many of them in high places, have paid for it. You will face heartache and loneliness. So will your children. They will suffer even more than you will suffer. There has been some progress in racial tolerance in the last few years, some acceptance of interracial marriage—but not enough. There are still many who do not understand how a man and a woman of different races can possibly love each other. Is your beloved a Christian? And how strong a Christian are *you?* Do you love each other in Christ, and are you strong enough in the Lord to love those who will criticize you and perhaps persecute you *and* your children? Will you teach your children to love those who will insult you and who will say fearful things to them? If you can do all this, take all this, if you sincerely feel that you are meant for each other and called of God to serve Him together and to serve your fellow man in love—then I must give you my blessing. But be *sure.*

A mixed marriage takes a lot of doing—a lot of being in the Lord. I know that many have tried it and failed. I know others who have made it work. To be absolutely honest, I know few black-white marriages that have made it; even among the best intentioned people, the pressures here have been just too much. But I have known missionaries who have come home with wives from another race—Orientals, Indians—who have found happiness and perfect understanding with each other; their radiant faces prove their love for God and for each other. At one Hollywood Christian group meeting I met a Christian missionary from India; a Caucasian woman, she was married to an East Indian Christian man. Their companionship was delightful, and it rejoiced my heart. I cannot quarrel with a marriage like that. They both had the mind which was in Christ; it was a union of two souls in their Redeemer—and it was beautiful.

Well, as the preacher said when he looked up at the clock, "This sermon has been longer than I thought it would be!" This discussion of the race problem has been longer than I planned—but I had to write it, had to get it down on paper, for I believe it to be the most crucial problem of our time. Albert Camus said, "We are all condemned to live together." I think we must all learn to live together in love and in peace, lest we all drown together in a holocaust of atomic dust.

9

Linda was going steady for some time before we realized it. She and Gary Johnson, a track star at school, were seeing no one else but each other and liking it. We came home late one night and heard her talking on the phone to Gary, long after she should have been in bed, and we realized then that things were really getting serious. Linda was too young for this. We wanted her to finish high school at least before thinking of marriage, so I took her to Kemper Hall in Wisconsin, where Cheryl had gone some years earlier. She didn't like it, but we believed it best for her and for Gary. She made excellent grades, and she was quite a young lady when she came home in June. We promised her that if she still wanted to marry Gary after she graduated, we would give our consent and any kind of wedding she wanted.

We planned it that way, but how often plans "Gang aft agley"! In October Linda and Gary announced that they had eloped to Las Vegas and been married, with Gary's parents as witnesses. Mad? I sure was—and then I remembered that I had done the same thing at an even earlier age. What could I say? I called Roy in New York with the news and he almost broke my eardrums as he shouted his objection. I knew he'd do that; I also knew that it would be better for him to get over his mad before he came home and faced the bride and groom.

Now our League was down to four—Dusty, Sandy, Dodie and Debbie—plus the dogs, cats, cows and horses.

When we moved to Chatsworth we found no Episcopal or Baptist churches, so we joined the Methodist Church. It was a good church. The pastor, Dr. Harold Hayward, baptized Debbie and Dusty, and we all went to work in the church school, choir, Vacation Bible School, M.Y.F. and in the adult organizations. There were some fine Christians in this church; the children adored Harold Johnson, the superintendent of the Sunday school. He had a gift for his job, and he knew his Bible and taught it well. The adult Bible class was stimulating and enjoyable, but the Sunday school lesson material sent to the church from national headquarters bothered me from the first; they seemed to lack any real Christian challenge. The great basic truths of Christianity—such as the atonement of the cross—were taken too much for granted, and were often ignored or treated too casually. I felt that the emphasis on social reform outweighed the emphasis on personal salvation through acceptance of Christ as Saviour, and that not nearly enough emphasis was put on personal, vital relationship with Christ.

We felt bad about another conflict in this church. Roy and I had participated in the Christian Anti-Communist Crusade at the Shrine Auditorium in Los Angeles, which was being conducted under the direction of Dr. Fred Schwartz, a man who was considered as something more than controversial by many church groups. Dr. Schwartz was a former Communist who had left the Party when he became aware of their plans for world domination and—principally, I think—because, following his conversion to Christ, he could not reconcile the faith of Christianity with the Godless, atheistic ideology of Communism. I despise godless Communism, and so does Roy. At the Shrine Auditorium we had given a brief Christian witness and we had commended the work of Dr. Schwartz. The very next day one of the leaders of the Methodist Conference in our area castigated Dr. Schwartz and his followers as rabble-rousers, and cautioned the congregation in our Chatsworth church to have nothing to do with anti-Communist movements of any kind. We thought this over carefully and prayerfully. When the Los

Angeles Annual Conference almost tied in voting
on whether the United Nations should admit
Red China, we felt that we had had it, and we
withdrew from the church.

That was then. As I think of it now, I think
we might not do now what we did at that time.
No church is perfect, no congregation is perfect and no two people in any congregation can
agree perfectly on everything. And people *are*
the church. Today, instead of running off to a
new fellowship, I think I would stand my
ground, as many of our friends in the Chatsworth Methodist Church wanted us to do. I
have at last learned to keep my own counsel
with God about many of the conflicts connected
with Christian faith. I have also learned that
Satan loves nothing better than a chance to split
every Christian fellowship on the face of the
earth; he loves to divide and conquer, and we
should think twice before helping him do *that*.

Different churches stress different aspects of
the truth. Some are sternly rock-bottom, insis-
tent on obeying every commandment laid down
in Scripture, in following every precept, in doing literally everything suggested in the Bible
and by the Christ. That is necessary, they believe, if we are to make it to heaven. Others
are not so strict or literal about this; the liberals
among us are not so much concerned with letter-
by-letter observance of the laws and ordinances
and commandments of Scripture as they are
with the application of Christian love in action
to the problems that confront us all. To use a
way-out illustration, the hippies (it might be

hard to call *them* Christian at all!) in their determination never to conform in any way to the orthodox Christian Establishment or to have anything to do with a literal interpretation of the Bible, still put on sandals (they call them "Jesus' boots"), wear shawls and insist that all they want to do is to love—and to *be* just plain love, as Jesus was. I have my doubts about the hippies, generally, but I think Billy Graham is right when he says that the Jesus' boots and the shawls and the insistence upon love among them are all indications of their search for truth which ultimately may lead them to Christ. I don't agree with them in many areas, but I would like to talk with them about Christ and His love, if that is really what they want. I would not run from them, nor from any way-out seeker.

Jesus did not flout the old Jewish Law; he fulfilled it; He superseded it with acts of love and mercy. In His mercy He fulfilled the love-thy-neighbor commandment of the Jews, even though it appeared to some of the strict Law observers of His day that He was breaking the Law. He came not to add to the Law, but to give us a grace and a power to live in such love that we would not need the constraints of the Law. Let me illustrate this.

Our agent, Joe Rivkin, was with us one night at a personal appearance in Anaheim, California. It was the night of Rosh Hashanah, the Jewish New Year, and, being of that faith, he felt uncomfortable—guilty—at the thought of working with us on this, his High Holy Day. During the intermission a little boy with cerebral palsy was carried into our dressing room by his distraught parents. Joe met them at the door where he was standing guard. He was supposed to keep people out, but he brought them in, with tears streaming down his face. I have never seen a deeper compassion on any human face. He saw to it that the whole family had choice seats for the rest of the show and he opened the gates of Disneyland for them to see everything there, *free!*

Now Joe is Jewish and I am Christian. When the little family had gone I said to him, "Joe, you have kept the highest law of God this day, loving and serving your neighbor as yourself. *Our* God will love that!" See what I mean? Different as we are in our various faiths and creeds and ideologies and theologies, we have this in common: we are all under orders to Go! Heal! Love! And we are to understand each other in love, as the Good Samaritan understood his Jewish sufferer on the road to Jericho.

We had intended to visit several churches before placing our membership but we visited only one. We found The Chapel in the Canyon in Canoga Park—an independent church with a Disciples of Christ background. One visit was enough; we knew that this was a church in which we could give a bold, vital witness for Christ. Its pastor, Larry White, had a passion for young people, and I liked that. He invited me to help with the choir—and I liked that. It wasn't long before we had choirs of children, teen-agers and adults singing the old, familiar hymns with new, lively arrangements. I was happy there.

I was more than happy when Billy Graham came to Los Angeles on a Crusade and the buses began to roll from the Chapel to the Coliseum. The Chapel went all-out in cooperation with Billy. It was in the Coliseum on Youth Night that Dusty, Sandy, Dodie and Debbie went down the aisle and gave their hearts to Christ. In that one moment, the memories of years of pain and hurt and sorrow were washed out of my heart. All four of them had been baptized previously, but Dusty and Sandy asked for immersion at the Chapel. (Dusty has *really* been baptized with water: he was christened at six months of age, sprinkled at seven in the Methodist Church, and immersed at the Chapel as a teen-ager!)

A lot of things happened in the summer of 1963. Our family was growing by leaps and bounds; I had always wanted a large family—and believe me, I got it! Grandchildren made their appearances so fast that I had trouble keeping track of them. One grandchild was born with trouble. Tom and Barbara had three girls—Mindy, Julie and Candy who became a diabetic at the age of sixteen months. That was hard for all of us to take—after all we had been through. Tom inspired and helped us, with a really Christian approach to the problem. He gave up his teaching job in Yreka, California, at the beginning of the school year, and brought his family back to Los Angeles where Candy could get good diabetic treatment at Children's

Hospital. As I watched him I saw a dramatic Christian faith demonstrated right before my eyes.

"I don't know where I'll find a teaching job in October that will pay enough to support my family," said Tom, "but God does, and He will take care of it." And take care of it God did. Shortly after Candy entered the hospital, Tom received a call to apply for an excellent teaching post in the Glendale School District. He got it—a far better job than the one he had left. I have seen it with this little family time after time. They never ask questions when adversity strikes; they simply trust God and do whatever has to be done without a murmur. God has come through for them every time. They are faithful—and He rewards that faithfulness. Many a time they have not had money enough to meet current expenses, but when their salary checks come in they give God a tenth of it, in tithe—and from somewhere, or from Someone, they find help to make a little more, or they get an extension of credit. It has always worked that way with them.

If I sound like a doting mother, forgive me. I reckon I am a doter, for God has given me much to dote on. He has given me Tom and Barbara and their three children—a family beautifully Christian. This has been a wondrous revelation and assurance that the promises of God are valid. He has given me thirteen grandchildren and one foster grandchild. Cheryl has two girls, Lisa and Kim, and two boys, Brian and Mark. Marion has a girl, Laurie, and two boys, Danny and David. Linda has a girl, Sherry, a boy, Robbie, and a foster-son, Victor. Dusty and his Linda have a girl, Shawna.

All of the children are now married. Dodie was married last fall to a staff sergeant in the United States Air Force, and will be residing on the East Coast until his duty is over, when they plan to return to California to live. Who knows how big our family will be by this time next year! Am I happy!

Late that summer we decided to take our four young children on a camper trip. Have you ever taken a camper trip with four young ones? If you haven't, you haven't lived! It is exciting, exhausting—and fun. We had a custom-built camper complete with tents, folding cots, a little picnic table with seats attached, a good cookstove and a kerosene lantern. You might call that trip a "roar," for it was the noisiest and most exciting trip this family of ours ever took. We roared down the Snake River, from Jackson Hole, Wyoming, in two big rubber rafts—the girls, a guide and I in one, Roy and the boys and another guide in the other. This was white water (rapids) and believe it or not Roy and the boys fished all the way downstream! What's more, they caught trout—and I had to fry them. They fished, too, in Yellowstone Lake, surrounded by bears and geysers and the most enchanting scenery in the world.

Roy did all the driving, and he drove like Jehu. We took turns sitting in the big double-bed bunk overhanging the truck cab; the kids fought for a place up there because it was a beautiful observation deck. I spent a lot of time up there, too, marveling at the landscape in the park that defies description. I found myself repeating Psalm 104. How in Yellowstone Park could anyone doubt the existence of God? I can't imagine anyone with enough arrogance to do that! Driving through the breathtaking Shoshone Canyon to Cody, the words of Habakkuk 3:19 raced through my mind as we wound along a road cut out of the side of the mountain, along high, sheer cliffs with no outside rails and with drops of hundreds of feet to the bottom: "The Lord God is my strength, and he will make my feet like hinds' feet, and he will make me to walk upon mine high places. . . ." It was like walking a tightrope—like the often narrow, perilous way of the Christian, when the eyes must look straight ahead and not *down,* if he is to see the unexpected obstacles that may be just around the bend. Yes, we had a roaring time of it in that canyon!

But I spent most of my time below—watching the pots and pans on the rattling stove. Every time Roy put on the brakes I made a dash to keep everything from sliding off the stove onto the floor. I sat there and thought of those pioneer women traveling through the same country in their covered wagons, and I did *not* envy them. But how I respected them! What Americans they were!

We ran into roaring storms in the Grand Canyon country. One storm ripped a hole as big as your washtub in the boys' tent (they were sleeping out that night), and they came into the camper soaked to the skin and covered with thick, red mud. Some of it was still with us when we got home.

The kids went along with us when we played the Seattle Exposition later that year. They got wet all over, all of them, all over again, when we had to play in the rain. It was all very uncomfortable—and it was all good for all of us. The family that goes through such experiences as these can go through *anything*—and I mean anything!

I got a phone call one morning at the motel in Seattle from a Reverend Harold Bredesen, a Dutch Reformed Minister from New York City. He invited me to have breakfast with him and Reverend Dennis Bennett, the rector of an Episcopal Church in Van Nuys, California. I didn't know quite what it was all about, but I had enjoyed breakfasts and luncheons with other clergymen who were interested in our witness, so I had breakfast with them the next morning. When the usual informal chitchat was over, they got down to business. They asked me if I had received "the in-filling of the Holy Spirit." A little surprised, I told them that I had been baptized by immersion at ten, had definitely been born again at thirty-five, and that I had experienced the Presence of the Holy Spirit twice during Robin's life. They accepted that, but they explained that there was a "second blessing"—a baptism "as by fire"—available to the seeking Christian. The hair on the back of my neck started to rise, and a warning whistle blew; this, I suspected, was "speaking in tongues" experience, and I had shied away from such way-out experiences, for I had been taught that the gift of tongues and speaking in tongues was not vital to salvation. These gifts, I believed, did not belong to this dispensation, but only to that of the disciples in the early Church, and then for a very special reason. Sitting at the breakfast table, I recalled the days—and nights—when I went with my parents and relatives to sit outside a Holy Roller church in Arkansas to listen to the strange goings-on inside. People in there, we were told, in their frenzy would grasp hot oil lamps in their bare hands; the shouting that came through those windows was deafening—and, I thought, a bit too much.

I told the two clergymen that I wanted no part of this second baptism and in-filling of the Spirit. I tried to explain my position to these obviously sincere, intelligent and completely dedicated men of God. I felt that God had called me to be simply a witness as an entertainer to all entertainers and churches and religious persuasions, and that since this charisma business had become such a controversial issue, my involvement in it might curtail the influence of my witness.

They asked then if they might pray with me. Inside I thought, "Here? In this restaurant?" Audibly I agreed. We bowed our heads and they started to pray for me and for my witness. Immediately, I felt the thrust of a great power behind their words, and it stirred me deeply. I felt strangely moved by it—when suddenly one of the men began to talk beautifully in a strange, foreign language which I could not understand. I pulled back, putting on the brakes.

When they finished, I thanked them and promised that I would try to attend one of their Full Gospel meetings. Roy and I had witnessed at a Full Gospel meeting at Disneyland, some years before this, and we had attended a similar Assembly of God meeting at Tulsa, Oklahoma, while on tour. We had both agreed then that we must respect these people who felt their religion so warmly and deeply, but that somehow, it was not for us, or within the frame of our religious thinking.

When I got back to my room, I wanted to pray. I dropped to my knees by my bed and told the Lord that if He wanted me to have this strange gift of tongues, I was ready to accept it. Immediately I felt a great, burning joy, and a sense of being lifted. I wanted to speak to God of what I felt, but I could not find the right words. I said, "Father, if it is Your will, let the Holy Spirit use my tongue to praise You."

A strange sound came from my throat—a sound completely foreign to me—then more—and more—jumbled, but after a few seconds coming more smoothly in a pattern of flowing speech. There was a great sense of power in it, an elation, a thanksgiving, and it was almost as though I would burst with it. I heard footsteps in the hall outside.

I stopped it, quenched it, cut it off. Perhaps I was fearful of Roy's reaction and I was sure this was Roy coming down the hall. It wasn't.

The footsteps were not his, and I felt a little foolish, being so afraid in the midst of such an overwhelming experience. I was also thinking, "This is too much. This is dangerous business— and it is not for me. Neither Roy nor the rest of my family will understand; they will think I have lost my mind, *and they will not listen any more to my witness.*"

I thanked God for the experience, and decided not to pursue it further.

We had another experience at the Seattle Exposition that shook us up—and strengthened us. Roy and I, the Sons of the Pioneers and Cliff Arquette had signed for thirteen hour-long shows for ABC Television, the first of which was to be filmed at Seattle. Our closing number was "How Great Thou Art," that wonderful song sung by Bev Shea at Billy Graham's meetings. Roy and I sang it standing under one of the beautiful arches of the Science Building, with great fleecy clouds as a backdrop. Just before we started to do the first take on the number, Art Rush got a call from the powers-that-be on the network, ordering us to delete the word "Christ" from the third verse of the song. We refused, just as we had refused to take out the cross on light thrown on the turf in Madison Square Garden when Roy sang "Peace in the Valley" some years before. The pressure was really put on us, but we were adamant about it. Later we found that our refusal to delete His name was one of the factors that cancelled out our show at the first option.

What does Christ say about such things? He

says, ". . . let him . . . take up his cross daily and follow me" (Luke 9:23). He also says that those who follow Him may be persecuted for their loyalty to Him. So? Think of what He went through to give us eternal life. How paltry is a television contract in comparison with *that!* He said that with every temptation to waver in doing right He would give us a way of escape. Though Roy and I have lost out more than once in secular work and opportunities, we have never gone hungry. When one door has been slammed in our faces, another has always opened. We have found Him completely honest in His promise. ". . . I will never leave thee, nor forsake thee" (Hebrews 13:5). He will be with us, whatever happens. He has said so, and I believe Him.

There are those who say, "Well, why does God give so many breaks to the disgusting, wicked people who ignore or hate Him? Why does He let them get away with theft, lying, murder—everything? Why does He let everything go so great for them, when some Christian like you gets the book thrown at him when he tried to do right?" I have found the answer to that question in the Seventy-third Psalm. Read it, and you will have the answer, too. In London, Billy Graham advised Roy to read this psalm when Roy asked him the same question. *Read it!* "When I thought to know this, it was too painful for me, Until I went into the Sanctuary of God; then understood I their end" (vs. 16, 17). The end of the wicked, that is—the wicked, who are cut off at last with no hope.

Read of the assurance held out to the faithful Christian: "Nevertheless, I am continually with thee: thou hast holden me by my right hand. Thou shalt guide me with thy counsel, and afterward receive me to glory" (vs. 23, 24).

That's good enough for me.

By the time we got back to Los Angeles it was time for the children to start school and for the adults to start taping a series for ABC. Two blows hit us in quick succession. The smog of L.A. hit me in the throat, and I had the same old trouble making myself speak above a whisper—and again God brought me through it. Then the Cuban crisis came. It looked like war, and none of us liked that. Poor Debbie was frightened almost out of her wits. She had memories of the war in Korea, memories planted in her mind as a baby—many memories. She came running to Roy one day.

"Daddy, are we going to have a war?"

"Honey, we hope not, but if we do, we must be ready for it."

She burst into tears: "Please, Daddy, I don't want a war. Please—*please!*"

She listened to us discuss the building of a bomb shelter on the ranch, and it terrified her.

I have seen much of war and its disastrous consequences in my lifetime. I hate it. War is hell on earth—the devil's business, not God's. I worry often over the words of Jesus, "And ye shall hear of wars and rumors of wars . . ." (Matthew 24:6). He said that because He knew the heart of man, and the ways of Satan with the heart of man. My Bible tells me that

194

"the heart . . . is desperately wicked; who can know it?" (Jeremiah 17:9). I know this: the heart of unregenerate men is capable of *anything*. Only the grace of God can tame the human heart. When man refuses to acknowledge the only One who can bring peace to the human heart, then war *is* inevitable. God in the heart is the Author of peace; Satan is the author of confusion.

I have wrestled with war much as a Christian. I wrestled with it in that moment with Debbie, and I was to wrestle with it even more horribly in the days that lay just ahead, though I did not know it then. I am torn by the thought that all of us must ". . . Go ye into all the world, and preach the Gospel to every creature" (Mark 16:15)—and by the thought that war is terribly anti-God and anti-Christian. Yet, when war comes with those who would impose godlessness and atheism on the world—then what are we who believe in God and Christ to do? Are we to stand by and see the great commission torn to shreds?

What can we do, as Christian individuals, to bring peace on earth? We can, as the old song says, "Let peace begin with me." We can live like Christians in our everyday walk, in every small thing and matter. We can let our light so shine in the little crises of life that it will penetrate into the bigger places—so infuse men and this world with the light of Christ, the Prince of Peace, that war will be impossible.

Only He and His Light can bring the peace we pray for.

10

Maybe I have mis-titled this book; perhaps it should be called "Trouble, Testing and Triumph," for that is the story of my life, after all—and it may be the story of your life, too. The year 1964, especially, was like that.

In 1964 the Religious Heritage of America chose me for their Churchwoman of the Year Award. That was good! I was invited to speak at the World's Fair in New York; that was good, too, and a prominent lay evangelist came to The Chapel in the Canyon and led a speaking-in-tongues service. In spite of my resolve to stay clear of such meetings, this one really gave me a joy I had never experienced before. It is impossible to explain it, but it was there. I was left more puzzled than ever about this form of worship.

This was the year Roy had a bad time of it in the hospital—and that was bad. He had been complaining of severe neck pains for some time, and the doctors found that three vertebrae were jammed together because of worn discs, and only an operation could correct it. His almost furious physical activity over the years—riding, racing speedboats in the ocean (that is really tough!), motorcycling, mountain climbing, hunting bobcats and bear—well, what could we expect? To the hospital he must go.

Just before he went, he insisted that I go to Hawaii with the children. We had promised them this a long time ago, and we felt that it would be good to go before Roy's confinement in the hospital. I'm glad we went, for I learned two very important things in Hawaii.

One was that Sandy was fascinated with every sailor, soldier and marine he met—and he met a lot of them. He spent most of his days with them on the beach, and I saw for the first time one of the major interests of his life. A burning desire to enlist took hold of Sandy on that beach.

Dusty liked the shops, the curios, the flowers —and the hula dancers! Dodie got sick again, and had to rest a lot. Debbie . . . ah, Debbie! She seemed a part of Hawaii, from the first day. I can still see her standing in the bow of a sailboat, her hair blowing in the breeze, her

eyes closed in ecstacy. She loved everything and
everybody in Hawaii; the music of this lovely
land answered the music in her heart. Debbie
was barely twelve, that year, but as I looked at
her I realized that she was no longer a child.

Roy's operation went well; he was on the
operating table for five hours, and a week after
the operation a staph infection frightened us,
but he slowly started to mend. We brought him
to the convalescent home in Bel Air August
14th, the day after Debbie's birthday. When
Debbie went to see her daddy, she was all
dressed up in clothes she had picked out herself. (She had begun to question Mama's taste
in clothes!) She was almost as tall as I was—
exuberant, tireless, a frolicking filly who gave
promise of tremendous energy and speed. I
was not at all sure that I was going to keep up
with her and I worried about her easy familiarity
with strangers. I thought with a pang, "It won't
be long before she leaves us; she looks more like
eighteen than twelve right now." She was no
longer interested in twelve-year-old children—
or twelve-year-old ideas; she loved to sit and
talk with adults.

Debbie sang in the church choir that Sunday
morning, and her face was radiant. How *alive*
she was! The radiance could have been due, in
part, to the fact that she was going on a bus ride
with her friends from the church to an orphanage in Tijuana, to take a load of gifts to the
children out there; but I think it was mostly
the radiance that comes to every girl when she

realizes that she is becoming a young lady. Either way, her face was pure joy.

Halfway through the service she caught my eye and motioned toward Dodie, who sat across the aisle from me. Dodie's face was as white as chalk; she looked at me and whispered, "Mama, I'm sick." When we got her home after the service, we told Debbie that the bus trip was off. That hurt; she pleaded tearfully, and she told us that her two young friends, Kathy and Joanne Russell, couldn't go if she didn't go. We relented. Come Monday morning, she and the Russells climbed into the bus and waved good-by. Good-by!

I spent most of that day with Roy at the Bel Air Convalescent Home. Driving home over the San Diego Freeway at about 3:30, I was deep in thought about many things—about our family, our health problems, about the house and the growing children. For once I hadn't turned on the car radio—thank the Lord! If it had been on, I would have gone berserk. As I turned into the driveway at the ranch, I saw Ruth Miner ("Granny," to the children) looking at me strangely. I parked the car and walked toward the house. The wind was swift and hot, blowing leaves into the dining room behind me.

"Ruth!" I exploded, "It's stifling in here. Why haven't you turned on the air conditioner?"

She walked over to me, took my arm and led me into the living room.

"Dale," she said, "Get hold of yourself. Something has happened. The bus had an accident after it left San Diego. Debbie and Joanne Russell are with the Lord."

I looked at her blankly. "With . . . the *Lord?*"

Then like the blow of a hammer, it struck into my brain. She was telling me that Debbie had been killed.

I screamed, "No! No! Not my baby, again!" I pounded the door with my fists. "Jesus! Jesus! *Help* me!"

Dusty walked in at that moment from the Chapel. He grabbed me and shook me violently. "Mom! You've told me to trust Jesus, as long as I can remember. If you meant that, you'd better start trusting Him right now. Debbie is OK. She's with Him!"

Thank you for that, Dusty. I needed it, in that moment.

The doctor came and gave me a sedative. I looked around for Dodie; she was nowhere to be seen. They found her huddled in a knot with her dogs in the rocks back of the house, sobbing her heart out. Through her tears she asked me, "Mom, are the angels jealous?" I suspected that she was remorsefully remembering the times when Debbie bested her in different situations and Dodie had been resentful of her—which was natural. Somehow I managed to tell her that the angels were never jealous, that in heaven there is nothing to make anyone unhappy and Debbie was in a place far better than the place *we* were in.

Asked Dodie, "Could you . . . get me another sister?" I said it was too early to even think about that.

All of a sudden I thought of Roy—and of the little portable TV set in his room. He watched it all day long! I dragged myself to the telephone to call the nurse, and Art Rush answered. He said that the news media had promised not to release anything on Debbie's death until I had been told. Bless them, forever!

The phone began ringing. The press, friends.
. . .

The phone at the Chapel was going crazy, too. Dusty and Sandy were helping there, as the frantic fathers and mothers who had children on the bus called and came in person. It was a nightmare. I clung to hope, like the drowning man clinging to a straw. I refused to accept her death. Maybe there was some mistake . . . maybe. . . . There was no mistake. The coroner in San Diego called and told me that Ernestine White (our minister's wife) had identified Debbie and Joanne. It was then that I called my mother in Texas and told her. She came by the next plane.

Friends poured into the house—Pat O'Shea, Judy Whisenant, so many others! They helped: I slowly regained control, and "got a new seat in the saddle."

Roy's surgeon told him. He told Art Rush later that the news sent Roy into a complete tailspin, and they had to rush him back to the hospital in Los Angeles. No wonder! Debbie was the one who had always met him at the door with a kiss and a smile; she was the one who took off his boots, rubbed his aching neck and brought him coffee. She and Dodie often took turns combing Daddy's hair, trying different hair styles while he watched TV. I think, perhaps, that Debbie was closest to her Daddy. One of the women at the church who had charge of Debbie's team that day said that just before the tire blew, hurling Debbie and Jo-anne into eternity, she had complimented Debbie on her new short summer haircut. Debbie said, "Mommy likes it short for the summer, but Daddy likes it long, and I'm going to let it grow out right away for him." Debbie had also asked special prayers for her Daddy that day.

In the middle of the night I was awakened by a loud, anguished moaning. It sounded like Debbie, until I remembered. Then I thought it might be Ruth Miner. I stumbled down the hall to her room and found her wide awake, too. She thought it was I who was moaning. We went to investigate and found Bowser, our dog, in a big chair in the living room, his head hanging over the seat, sobbing like a stricken human being. Ruth went back to bed and I went to the altar in our living room.

I lighted the candles and looked down at the huge family Bible which was open. My eyes fell on the words of Paul to the Hebrews, in Chapter Twelve: "If ye endure chastening, God dealeth with you as with sons; for what son is he whom the father chasteneth not? But if ye be without chastisement whereof all are partakers, then are ye bastards and not sons. Furthermore, we have had fathers of our flesh which corrected us, and we gave them reverence; shall we not much rather be in subjection unto the Father of spirits and live? For they verily for a few days chastened us after their own pleasure; but he for our profit, that we might be partakers of his holiness. Now no chastening for the present seemeth to be joyous but grievous; nevertheless afterward it yieldeth the peaceable fruit of righteousness unto them which are exercised thereby. Wherefore, lift up the hands which hang down and the feeble knees; and make straight paths for your feet, lest that which is lame be turned out of the way; but let it rather be healed" (Hebrews 12:7–13).

What does this mean: "lest that which is lame be turned out of the way"? I believe it refers to those Christians who are watching the professing Christians in time of deep trouble, who might be attracted to the Way—and watching to see if it really works in life. If the Christian fails to demonstrate the power and grace of God in extremity, that person might be turned from the Way, thinking that the Way is not adequate to meet the vicissitudes we are all called upon to meet.

I read it, and I was strengthened; I was aware of the Presence of God within and around me. The psalmist said, "Examine me, O Lord, and prove me" (Psalm 26:2). He is the Word; He was in Paul, talking to those Hebrews, and He was talking straight to me now. I knew it; I felt it, and I heeded His words. I went back to bed, confident that He would "perfect that which concerneth me" (Psalm 138:8). I knew He was going to be with me all through what was ahead. He had promised: "Lo, I am with you *always* . . ." (Matthew 28:20).

And He was with me—all through it. If he had not been with me, I could never have gotten through it. He was with me when I went to see Roy in the UCLA Medical Center, and from there to Forest Lawn to make the funeral arrangements. I had to make arrangements all by myself; the Russells were with their other daughter, Kathy, who had been hurt in the accident. The rest was up to me. When I tried to get up from my chair in Roy's room at the hospital, I hardly made it. I felt wooden.

And He was with me at Forest Lawn, as I picked out the two caskets, and the flowers, and made arrangements for the services. Mrs. White, our pastor's wife, would give the eulogy, since her husband (who had been on the bus) was still in the hospital in Oceanside. The attendant at Forest Lawn explained that the coroner had advised that under no circumstances were the caskets to be opened.

The next day Mother, Art Rush, my friend Judy Whisenant and I drove out there again. Art talked briefly with the man in charge, and came back to me shaken and agitated. "Dale," he said, "I have been asked to make a decision here that I simply cannot make. They tell me that they think you can and should see Debbie, but it has to be your decision. They have worked very hard to make her presentable, and . . . ."

I made the decision immediately. I would not make the mistake again I had made in refusing to look at Robin and I went in with the Russell family—and with God—to look at my baby. I saw a pretty, sleeping young girl dressed in the white dress she had worn at her sixth-grade commencement, with a pink bow in her lustrous black hair, her long slender fingers clasping a little blue stuffed animal she had won at Pacific Ocean Park on Saturday. She looked about eighteen. I stood there with her, knowing that my real Debbie was in eternity—*and in that moment I was with her in eternity, out of the body, in the Spirit.* There are no words to describe this experience; one has to go through it himself to understand it.

I fell to my knees and thanked God for the nine years He had let us have Debbie. I told Him that I trusted Him with her, and I committed her into His hands. I got up and walked out of that place. God walked with me. He had not left me desolate. He had come to me and taken my heartbreak into His own heart. When I reached the house in Chatsworth a friend said to me, "Dale, your face is positively *glowing;* it is . . . radiant. How . . . ?" Only God could do it. He kept the radiance there all through the services that followed. He had removed from me forever all fear of death.

The following Sunday He gave me the strength to speak briefly at the Chapel about the great truth of His everlasting arms, about His being ". . . a very present help in time of trouble" (Psalm 46:1).

Of course there were painful moments after that. That is to be expected, for death always means the loss of the presence of the loved one who leaves us. It is the end of a personal, physical relationship that is hard to bear. A week after the funeral I went into Debbie's closet—too soon!—to see what I could do about her clothes. Staring at those clothes, I realized that the little laughing Debbie would never wear them again, and momentarily I went to pieces. I ran into the kitchen, reached for a cup of coffee and turned to see my mother. She saw my pale face, my trembling hands. She heard me say, "It isn't right! It isn't fair! Why did it have to happen? She had a brilliant future before her, and it was all snapped off, just like *that!* *Why?*"

She looked me in the eye and let me have it. "I'm surprised and disappointed in you. You know better than to give way to this. *What's happened to your faith?*"

I deserved it; I had asked for this. I was humbled and ashamed, and I asked the forgiveness of God. He seemed to be standing there, waiting to forgive. In perfect peace I went first to our family altar and then to my desk. No, He *led* me to my desk. I picked up my pen and asked Him to guide it as I wrote about Debbie —as I had written about Robin. I had to get this down on paper, for the benefit of other mothers who might lose other Debbies.

It poured from my pen for hours, for days. I could not stop writing; I could do nothing else, think of nothing else, until it was a finished book. We called it, *Dearest Debbie,* and we dedicated it and donated its royalties to World

Vision, Inc.—Bob Pierce's organization, through which Debbie had come to us from Korea.

Roy came home, his neck in a big steel brace. When Christmas came, we sang a song together, "Happy Birthday, Gentle Saviour," at the Music Center in Los Angeles for Teen World Opportunity. I was never prouder of him.

God was with us there, too!

11

Early in January Sandy told us he wanted to enlist in the army. He had asked us for our consent to enlist a year previously, when the Viet Nam affair was developing so quickly. We had refused then, for we wanted him to finish high school. Now he said, "I want to serve my country. I want to prove myself a man. I promise you that I will get my high-school diploma in the service." He was engaged to a lovely girl who attended the Chapel services with him, and we asked him about that, and about her. He said she had promised to wait for him.

We gave our consent. This time his courage and determination were too much for us. Off he went to Fort Polk in Louisiana. I went to see him graduate at Polk and watched him march in review with his company, and I was proud—proud of this boy who was making such a gallant fight against his handicaps, proud of his love of the flag and of his desire to keep that flag flying. He volunteered to go to Viet Nam—and was turned down. Instead he was assigned to the tank corps and sent to Germany. As a matter of fact, he volunteered twice for Viet Nam, but they wouldn't let him go. His officers said to him, "Your family has suffered enough; we are sending you to Germany." Later they told us that his reflex actions were just too slow for hand to hand combat.

So our Sandy went off to Germany, and we went out to a new home in Apple Valley, where Roy had leased the Apple Valley Inn. Apple Valley is in desert country, and that was good for me, with my bronchitis and touch of asthma. I took to desert life with ease; the glorious early mornings and late afternoons were balm from heaven! We joined the (Presbyterian) Church of the Valley, where Dodie began taking instruction for membership. Dusty had a number of friends in nearby Victorville High School who attended the High Desert Baptist Church, so he went there. He was in his senior year of high school; Dodie was in the eighth grade.

We bought an old adobe house near the Inn, a house shaped like a horseshoe with a big backyard that was perfect for our menagerie: Bullet,

Bowser, Bobo, Bambi (our Chihuahau), Sugar (half bobcat and half just plain cat) and Smokey (proud Persian cat). It is a happy house and we have found great happiness in it. It isn't fancy, but it is adequate—and a constant challenge to experiment. I was born an experimenter with houses. Roy says I'm a natural furniture mover, forever changing things around—so much so that he never knows where to sit down! We painted it a forest green with white trim, and it stands there in a desert devoid of any other green, like an oasis. We love it.

Let me tell you about Smokey. While Debbie was still with us, she begged for a kitten. We said no, because we knew what could and probably would happen to a kitten in a house full of cat-hating dogs. I am still haunted and hurt by the memory of Debbie's tears when we told her she couldn't keep a kitten given her by one of our neighbors. We already had a big black tomcat we called "Knight," a pitiful rack of bones who had to be thrown bits of food up on the roof of the house because our cat-despising dogs wouldn't let him come down. We finally coaxed him down and took him away to a dairy, where he got plenty of milk for the rest of his life. After that, we vowed there would be no more cats.

But two weeks after Debbie's death this big Persian cat ambled into the kitchen door (left open in a moment of carelessness) and Dodie promptly gave him a saucer of nice fresh milk. I scolded her, for I knew what would happen. It happened. The Persian refused to leave the

House of Rogers. I set myself for war between cat and dogs, and it came—but it didn't end as I expected. This cat was no amateur in battle. When a dog took just one step in his direction, he made a flying leap to the back, head or neck of the startled dog, dug his claws in and rode the dog until he yelped "Uncle." Smokey did that to every dog in the place in turn. Soon all was peace and love and understanding. Even Roy, who had never liked cats, became a Smokey fan. If Debbie could only have seen *that!*

Late in October I went to Texas to spend my birthday with my mother. On the thirty-first of the month, I had a dream that shook me badly. I dreamed that I saw a rider galloping full speed across a wide plain, heading straight for me. Suddenly his horse stumbled and fell and they rolled over and over in the sand. The horse got up, but the man didn't; he lay there motionless, and I knew that he was dead. I woke up with a scream.

I was terribly depressed all the next morning, even as I sang in church and gave a brief testimony. Late in the afternoon the whole family had dinner with me at Waxahachie, in celebration of my birthday, but I didn't feel like celebrating. I had that feeling of detachment and suspension again—that other-world feeling. I felt that something had happened, or was about to happen, that would change my life. I wondered, uneasily, if one of us around that table was in danger—perhaps in danger of death.

On Monday I flew back to Los Angeles.

Marion was to meet me at the Los Angeles airport for coffee. Marion was there—and Cheryl was with her, and there was an odd look on their faces. Sensing some kind of undercurrent, I sang out, "Do we have a problem, kids?"

Cheryl replied, soberly and carefully, "Sort of, Mom."

The panic signal went up. In rising fear I asked, "Who is it?"

Cheryl said, "Mom, it's Sandy. He's gone."

My voice started to rise, uncontrollably, and I shouted, "What do you mean—gone? Sandy isn't in Viet Nam. He's in Germany!"

Dusty and Roy came and took me by the arms and Dusty said gently, "I know, Mom. Sandy was at a party Saturday night," (the man on horseback in my dream!) "and some guys got him to drink a lot of hard liquor, and it killed him."

I almost fell to the floor. In the airport office Cheryl gave me a tranquilizer, and I heard the rest of the story. Sandy's body was to be flown home immediately after the military funeral in Germany, accompanied by an officer.

Once more—Forest Lawn. We arranged for a military funeral. Sandy was to be laid to rest in a crypt beside Robin and Debbie. When I went in to look at the boy who wanted so much to be a part of our country's action in Viet Nam, I almost cracked. There he lay in his beloved uniform—a private, first class, felled not by a bullet but by a bottle! In my heart raged bitter denunciation of the lack of regulations that would allow an eighteen-year-old private to be

213

served enough liquor to kill him. I was beside myself with sorrow and anger for this boy who had tried so hard to measure up—to prove himself a man even in a drinking bout!

The officer who had brought Sandy's body all the way from Germany sat down with me and told me how it had happened.

He told me how hard Sandy had worked on a three-week maneuver in Germany to earn his first-class stripe, and how overjoyed he was the day he got it. He was tired out that night, too tired for the wetting-down-the-stripes party in which his buddies participated. That sort of party wasn't meant for Sandy; he was no drinker, but this was a custom in the service, and he went along with it. Spurred on by his pals, and not wishing to be a wet blanket—and to prove himself a man—he drank with the rest of them. He strangled from this overdose of liquor to which his body was not accustomed. The boys in the service use all sorts of tricks to get liquor, and the officers were almost powerless to stop it, much as they disliked it. Sandy wasn't the first victim of this sort of thing, and he probably will not be the last.

After a while, I calmed down. I remembered the last letter Sandy had written, telling us how grateful he was for the Christian home he had enjoyed, how he believed in God and his country and his flag, and how anxious he was to get to Viet Nam. It hurt me that he didn't get there, because I was sure he would have preferred death there to death with that bottle. I apologized for my outburst and went back to touch his hand and to thank God that Sandy was a Christian. As I stood there I saw that God had led Sandy to prove himself as a first-class private, that he had known the love of a fine girl whom he planned to marry, and that in his death he might be spared future frustration and heartache as he struggled with his handicaps. The fact that he had died in such an ignominious manner in no way nullified what he had accomplished. We had been surprised that he passed the army physical and made it through boot camp; now we were proud of him. I did not want to let him go. I almost broke when the flag was lifted from his casket, folded and presented to me. On the way out, I hardly saw anyone for my tears.

Just before Christmas we received a small package from his commanding officer in Germany; it was the wedding and engagement ring he had purchased for his beloved Sharon. She arranged to have a cross made of them. Sandy would have liked that.

That summer the USO asked us to do an entertainment tour in Viet Nam. We promised to go for two reasons: we wanted to go to Viet Nam as sort of substitutes for Sandy, who couldn't go; and we wanted to satisfy ourselves as to why the United States was engaged in this conflict. We almost didn't make it; my world started spinning again. The inner-ear infection was back. I couldn't keep my balance when I tried to walk, I vomited endlessly and was so ill that I was rushed off to the hospital. The Adversary whispered to me, "You don't want to go to Viet Nam. *You can't go!*" I gritted my teeth and said to God, "Lord, I am not trying to tempt You by demanding some sort of sign about this trip, but You know I can't go while I'm as sick as this. Do You want us to go? If You do, let my vision and my equilibrium and my stomach be normal in the morning." I went to sleep, and slept like a baby. In the morning I opened my eyes upon a hospital room and a world that was steady as a rock. The dizziness and the pain were gone.

We took our shots, and flew to Viet Nam.

The story of what happened to us in Viet Nam is written in detail in my little book, *Salute to Sandy,* and I will not repeat it all here. It is enough to say that it was one of the great strengthening experiences of our lives. We saw American youth at its best, its noblest; our hearts broke at the sight of their suffering, but our hearts sang a new song as we saw how they took it. There was no whimpering, no complaining; there was only a sense of duty and consecration in getting a mean and deadly job done. They knew it *had* to be done, whatever it cost. They were there to give everything they had, including their lives, to get it done. All the doubts I ever had about American youth disappeared as we entertained them, and talked with them, and visited them in the hospitals. We worked unbelievably long hours, doing what we could to help them, but what we did, compared with what they were doing, seemed so little! I would do it all over again, for Sandy, for the boys—and for the cause for which they were fighting and dying. I came home believing in that cause, and believing in them, and loving them.

It was exhausting, though: We came home dead tired to Apple Valley. I finished off the *Salute to Sandy,* which I had worked on in Viet Nam and in airplanes going there and coming back. I finished it, sent it off to the publishers and arranged with them to pay its royalties to the Campus Crusade for Christ, International. The book was published on Sandy's birthday; Campus Crusade is still benefitting from its sale.

It was hard, settling down after those days at the heart of the hurricane of war, but we had one blessed day that helped a lot. That was the day Dusty got married. Dusty had been working in a big supermarket in Middlefield, Ohio, with his close friend George White, whose family owned the business. Here he had fallen in love with Linda Yoder, a Middlefield girl. Roy wanted him to stay closer to home, and to find his lifework somewhere near us, or with us, but Dusty wanted to make it on his own, and we respected his decision. We went to his wedding.

I wept at the wedding—but for joy. I wept at the thought of another child leaving the Rogers' roost. It was not easy to let him go, nor was it, I think, easy for him to go. Nothing is ever easy for the children of people in public life. Somehow, there is always some pressure upon them, demanding that they measure up to what other people expect of them as the children of so-called celebrities. It is difficult for them to be individuals, to be human beings in their own right, to do what they want to do and to be what they want to be. We would miss our Dusty, but he deserved his chance to spread his wings in new territory.

There they stood—Dusty tall, broad-shouldered, and Linda, so tiny! She was radiant. Dodie was a bridesmaid—a vision in her long red empire velvet dress. Dusty's eyes widened in surprise as he watched her come down the aisle of the church—the scrawny little girl with the long dark pigtails who had played with him and wrestled with him and Sandy and Debbie. Even when he was wrong, she took his side! Memories soared in the hearts and ears and eyes of all of us.

So the last boy was married. He works today with the Yoder Construction Company in Middlefield, and does an occasional personal appearance with Roy at the openings of the Roy Rogers Chuckwagons (beef sandwiches) across the country. At home he idolizes his baby— Shawna Marie.

We came home then to Apple Valley—just we three.

12

We had moved to Apple Valley to "retire"—
to take it a bit easier, to slow down, to think
and rest and to do a lot of things we had never
had time to do in the busy past. Alas for all
that! We found ourselves as busy as ever. We
were still doing TV appearances; I was away on
speaking engagements much of the time; Roy
had his restaurant openings and his activity
with horse breeding—and the management of
the Inn was a heavy, heavy load.

It was just too much. We changed our relationship with the Inn, turning over the lease
and all managerial duties to the owners, but we

bought—outright—a big bowling alley across the street, and started converting it into our personal museum. Into it we put row upon row of photographs and scrapbook materials; Robin, Debbie, Sandy and Roy's mother each have a separate display, and there is an exhibit which we call "The Religious Heritage of Our Country." Good old Trigger, beautifully mounted, has a room of his own. When Roy had suggested, at the time of Trigger's death, that he would have him mounted "for posterity," I hooted and objected, but he had his way about it. Trigger was mounted and set up, and now I'm glad he was. The rapt expressions of the kids and grown-ups who visit the museum and look at him convince me that it was the thing to do. When Bullet and Buttermilk leave us, I have no doubt that they will also be readied for posterity by a taxidermist. Right now, they are not concerned about it. Buttermilk and Bullet are enjoying retirement, and they act as though they owned the whole place!

With the slowing of the pace I found time to think and evaluate much that has happened in our lives. I had time now to "sum up," to estimate our failures and our successes, to decide what had been good about it, and what had been bad. I have come to several conclusions about it all.

I have come to believe that *everything* in our lives which we had entrusted to God was good, and that those parts of it in which we tried to go it alone were (frequently) not so good. Like the woman at the well, we were happy when we let down our buckets into the Living Waters of God and Christ; when we did not, we were *not* happy. Yet even those years in which we tried to live without God were not wasted; He used them to work out His purpose in our lives. I am more than grateful for that. God runs a good school here on earth, and we who are His pupils get good marks only when we listen to Teacher!

And I have become more and more optimistic and hopeful about the future. Our past is prologue; we can and must build on it for tomorrow. I am confident that the future will be better than the past. "He holds the whole world in His hands." I rest on that.

I sum up with this: *I believe in the younger generation; I believe in our country; I believe in God.*

I love our young people. On the whole I think they are courageous, brave, honest and intelligent—and too often frustrated by too much permissiveness at the hands of overmaterialistic parents. Even though we do not always agree with them, the least we can do is to *listen* to them. Wisdom does not begin and end with parents; it is something that is passed down from generation to generation. Sometimes the kids are right and we are wrong. "Out of the mouth of babes and sucklings," says the psalmist, "hast thou ordained strength . . ." (Psalm 8:2)—and wisdom. Their world is hurtling into change after change—fast, too fast, and our young people are trying desperately to meet the changes at their level of understanding. Beneath

221

their rock-and-roll flamboyance they have a sur-
prising depth of understanding.

I realized this one day last spring, when
Dodie bounced into the kitchen, threw a sheet
of paper at me and said, in an offhand way,
"Wanna read something crazy?" and bounced
out again. I read it. Here it is:

TO WHOM IT MAY CONCERN: I was at
my typewriter wondering what to do next,
when all of a sudden my fingers started running over the keys. . . . Please bear with me
and my mistakes, because it's been so long. I am
also getting senile! My grandchildren seem to
think so, though I don't believe it for an instant.
Rather, with the end so near, I see things in a
different perspective. I still see a future, and
not a materialistic one—but a future that I
will not have to struggle through, as I have
struggled in the past. I am quick to point out
peoples' faults, but this is only because they
take life as if it were going to last forever.
There are times when my memory fails me,
but I can still remember so much more! My
eyesight is nearly gone, but I see more things
now than I've ever seen before, and though I
can't hear well I have heard what I should
have heard—and when I could have done
something about it. My fingers are not as
nimble now, and only through other hands
can my thoughts be conveyed.

Yes, I am what you call old and aged, but
soon I will once again be romping around. I
may look like a dried-up old prune, and these
wrinkles may tell a story, but I am so beautiful. It is too bad you do not understand. You

feel sorry for me when I hobble across the street or when your young men bump into me and spill my packages. You have even laughed at me in my good dress with that crooked little hat, but I feel no sorrow. If only you could have what I have! This young girl beside me knows nothing of what she will be or even what she wants to be when age permits her. Oh, yes, she may outrun me, but unless she awakens, as so many others ought to, she will never outlive me, nor outgo me. I have more energy to see the truth and have it revealed to me forever—but my body is decaying, as it must. All I have said is nothing, and yet it is everything. Look at me. You see an old woman. Look again. You see a young heart. A young soul! I have known sorrow, but comfort has always followed. No, I really have not much to say; how I do ramble on about nothing! I am growing weaker with each word that pours from my mouth, and soon I will be gone—but I will keep watch and know that I must not interfere. I will be rooting for the blind to see!

I say *that* is filled with wisdom. Here was a seventeen-year-old girl looking ahead to the day when she will be old. She has depth of perception; she stumbles a bit (don't we all?); she is reaching for something she can't quite understand or describe, but she is *reaching*. She is looking ahead, not back. She has no past, only a future—and she is deeply, spiritually concerned about it. I love her for that, as I love all youth.

Roy and I attended the high-school graduation exercises of our first grandchild, Melinda

Christine Fox. Mindy was an honor student and student-council officer, and she plans to continue her education at the Bible Institute of Los Angeles. Earlier she and another fine Christian girl had debated two atheistic boys on the subject, "Is God Dead, or Not?"—and the girls won, hands down.

At the commencement, however, Roy and I were distressed and saddened as we listened to two addresses by an obviously rebellious boy and girl. There was not a hint of gratitude to home, church, school or God for their accomplishments, not a shred of hope for the future —only condemnation and bitterness. They delivered their sour apples with a sure hand— brilliant and cutting, and it nearly ruined the whole commencement as far as we were concerned. One wonders, who in good conscience could have approved those addresses, free speech notwithstanding! It was obvious that the Adversary had had a field day with these two young people. The young lady was accurate when she said that they were leaving school totally unprepared to meet the challenges of this confusing world. I was sure that *they* were unprepared to meet any problem, if their words meant anything at all.

Someone had failed to give these intellectually gifted young people the undergirding of that vital relationship to God through Christ— wherein lies our hope of the future. Someone must *not* have shown them the real love of God, the true wisdom that is of God—that every good gift of life is the gift of God. The young man deplored the expenditure of money on arms and on space flights; in his opinion, our government was inexcusably responsible for the deaths of three astronauts in their flaming capsule. He will learn, as we all learn, that man is fallible and that sometimes his failures result in tragedy to himself and to others—but that is not the question! The question, in my mind, is why he did not spend some time discussing the dedication of the astronauts and of all the others involved in the tragedy. He missed that completely.

I could not help comparing the attitudes of these two young people with that of Mindy, Candy and Julie. At Christmastime they had a beautiful group photograph made in color of themselves holding their violins; they presented this to their parents, with a letter of appreciation, and a scrapbook of their lives together as a Christian family. The letter was a masterpiece of gratitude for the home and the hope they had been given by their parents. I am certain that the Christian character of all three of them is the result of their training in a home where Christ is an ever-present guest, where there is peace, purpose and challenge—and love. Tom found the Better Way years ago; it is transplanted in his children.

Yes, they and their parents, I am sure, will be called squares by some people, but I'll take their kind of square deal every time. The square young people will be the ones to survive and to conquer this jungle. I know that there are more squares in the ranks of youth than there are atheists. In them lies our hope—and God tells me that we will not be disappointed.

I believe in the squares among youth. I believe that their quiet faith in all that is good will outlast the ravings of our loudmouthed, sophisticated rebels, unwashed and unresponsible hippies, draft-card burners and sexual deviates. The squares are the majority; the others are the lunatic fringe. They will pass, and be forgotten.

I believe in my country. I *cannot* believe that God went to all the trouble of bringing the Pilgrims and other settlers to these shores and of guiding the building of the greatest democracy the world has ever seen, only to let it be destroyed. Just as He created man for eternal life, He created America for a purpose still to be worked out in a long, if distant, future. His one increasing purpose for this country must be and will be worked out in the dedicated lives of God-oriented Americans.

One morning in Houston a tall, handsome young man knocked on the door of our hotel room. He had heard our "Salute to God and Country," at the rodeo the night before. He had a clipping in his hand (he had walked across the city to bring it to us), which contained an article protesting the efforts of an atheistic group of people who were trying to eliminate the words "In God We Trust" from our coins. He was a marine just back from Viet Nam, with three bullet wounds in his body (a tough Texan!). I told him that we had just done a tour in Viet Nam in memory of a boy who could not go to the battlefront, and to satisfy our questions as to why we were fighting there. I asked him if he knew why we were there. He answered, "I thought I did, but a lot of folks here at home—even preachers—are saying we should not be there at all, and that we shouldn't even talk of God for fear of offending the Communists! I have told them that I would rather offend the Communists than the God who made them." Amen, soldier! He said that he was going back to Viet Nam as soon as he could. I thank God for that boy and for all others like him, who salute the flag instead of desecrating it, who love their country and are ready to die for it.

This nation's greatness depends upon her faith in the purposes of God. The whole world is watching and waiting to see if we shall keep that faith, or lose it. The Bible describes the only faith upon which we can continue to be strong and great when it says that "Righteousness exalteth a nation" (Proverbs 14:34); it also says, "Blessed is that nation whose God is the Lord" (Psalm 33:12). I think we *must* keep this awareness of God and His righteousness as our national foundation, if we are to endure.

Just after our three great astronauts, Anders, Borman and Lovell, circuited the moon and read from up there a part of the creation story in Genesis we took time out to salute and honor them during a show at the Astrodome. It was one of the great moments in the march of man and history—and the Bible was the only Book big enough to be read in that moment! God bless them for doing that—and God help us to do something more than just honor them for doing it! May we have the courage to stand by Him as the creator of our Republic, the courage and strength to work for it, fight for it, live for it and if necessary to die for it! That is the least we can do for God and country.

A good friend, Hal Southern (a country and western composer and musician), gets down to brass tacks on this question, and he says well what I would like to say to all America. Here is his declaration of faith in his country:

Some day in the not too distant future, historians and scientists will look at the physical and written remains of our present-day civilization and shake their heads in total disbelief, unable to comprehend how an advanced culture such as ours could totally disintegrate in a mass of crime, social strife, wars, welfarism and total lack of involvement of the people in their own destiny.

You would think, that in our present state of confusion, both national and international, we would take heed of the lessons of history. History does repeat itself and we are going through a phase of permissiveness, self-gratification, racial disintegration, violence and moral destruction that can only lead to self-destruction on a scale unparalleled in history.

Isn't it about time we stand up and be counted? Do we want the kind of a country where it is considered square to be patriotic, stupid to be honest, insane to follow the Golden Rule, where you are considered Establishment if you work hard, raise a family and pay your bills? Is it wrong to be clean, literate,

thrifty and have a short haircut? Is it wrong
to like country music, tunes that have a mel-
ody, lyrics that say "I love you," rhythms that
want to make you dance with a partner, or
are we square because we don't like ear-
shattering, wild, psychedelic sounds with ob-
scene lyrics and clothes to match?

This nation wasn't made great by unwashed
lazy hippies, crybaby welfarism or racial mi-
norities begging for a handout. This nation
was built on the honest hard work, thrift, guts,
desires and needs of Irish, Jew, Negro, Mexican, Chinese and endless other people. Common people who had the guts to be uncommon,
people of all races, creeds and nationalities,
people with one common bond—*freedom.* In
their hearts they must have known that America
was the last stand for the individual, the last
chance to justify man's existence on earth.

Is it wrong to ask that our communications
media be a little more impartial in its treatment of things patriotic? All too often, it seems
that some radio stations, for instance, will not
play anything they label as patriotic or controversial, but will turn around and play protest and anti-Establishment records all day
long. Is it controversial to say on record that
you like being an American, are proud to be
an American and that you will fight to the
death for the chance to continue being an
American?

Why should Capitalism, Free Enterprise and
Conservatism be dirty words? Is it so wrong
to want to make a profit on honest endeavors?
What is wrong with making money and re-
investing it in a strong America? This great
nation wasn't built on a cradle-to-the-grave

philosophy, nor will it survive with the government always acting as a big brother. Remember, Uncle Sam is your uncle—not your Dad!

Well, I insist on being counted. I'm four-square for Mom, Apple Pie, the Bible and the Flag. I'm for free enterprise, capitalism, do-it-yourself guts, less government in private enterprise and, last, but never least, I'm for freedom, a kind of freedom the whole world envies, a freedom that makes people all over the world risk their lives to achieve, a freedom that allows us the strength to have inscribed on the Statue of Liberty:

Give me your tired, your poor,
Your huddled masses yearning to breathe free,
The wretched refuse of your teeming shore.
Send these, the homeless, tempest-tossed to me.
I lift my lamp beside the golden door!

That says it, for me!

I believe in God, and in God in Christ. I believe in Them not only because I want to, but because I *have* to! Their power in my life and experience has been so overwhelming that, without Them, I would feel like an astronaut lost and wandering helplessly, forever in space. When a famous astronomer was asked why he believed in God, he replied, "How can anyone go out at night and look up at the stars and *not* believe in God?" He says it for me.

You know, I used to fly into a rage when I heard someone say, "God is dead." But I don't, any more. That crazy idea didn't last very long, did it? *It* seems to be dead now! Why did I ever worry about it? Why did I let myself get so mad? When God wearied of such chatter, He took care of it in His own way.

No, God isn't dead; neither is He obsolete. His laws are as certain and as eternal as His presence in the stars, in the universe around us —and as contemporary as the sun, the stars, the moon or the common winds that brush the cheeks of all of us. He is here, and He cares.

We deceive ourselves when we think of Him *only* as a God of love and forgiveness—great as all that is; and that He doesn't really care very much if and when we ignore His teachings; yes, and that we can go about committing every sin in the catalog and still be sure that, like a doting father with a spoiled child, He will forget and forgive us as though we had lived like saints. He is a God of *justice* as well as a God of mercy.

I believe what my Bible tells me—that we are made in the image of God. I do *not* believe that God is made in the image of man. Man cannot whittle Him down to man's size, much as man would like to do just that. You cannot test or analyze God; you cannot put Him in a test tube. He is *omnipotent* (all-powerful), *omniscient* (all-knowing), *omnipresent* (present everywhere, all the time). I read this about Him, in Psalm 139, "Whither shall I go from thy spirit? or whither shall I flee from thy presence? If I ascend up into heaven, thou art there; if I make my bed in hell, behold thou art there; if I take the wings of the morning and dwell in the uttermost parts of the sea, Even there shall thy hand lead me, and thy right hand shall hold me" (vs.

7–10). This isn't poetry, to me; it is truth and reality, *and it has been proved in my life's experience.* He has been with me when I passed through the hell of sorrow and suffering, many, many times; He was with me then, and He is with me now that I walk in a heaven-on-earth that is heaven because He is here with me, *now.*

In February of 1969 Roy and I faced a press conference in Houston. Press conferences are always ordeals; you never know what questions the reporters are going to throw at you. At this conference, one of them said to us, "You two people seem almost unreal, as though you had suddenly appeared out of a cloud in the West. Tell me: is it hard to be thought of as 'goody two-shoes'?" That set me back a bit, because never since God revealed my unworthiness to me in 1948 have I thought of myself as "good." I am certainly not good (even Jesus asked, in Matthew 19:17, "Why callest thou me good?"); and if there is anything about me that is at all acceptable in that sense, it is strictly due to my faith in Jesus Christ. Whatever good I do, He does through me.

Roy and I have those moments which every married man and woman have, when we are less Christian and less good than we should be. I would be less than honest if I said there had never been any squalls in my Christian walk or in our marriage. There have been tempests— but our house is built on the Rock, and it has stood firm through every squall and storm. We have grown together in our faith, and growing

is sometimes a painful process. But with it comes
—has come to us—a quiet, inner joy in knowing that by the grace of God we have learned
to accept ourselves and each other as God's
children and creation. As human creatures, we
still make mistakes, but our God makes no mistakes. He makes no two of us alike, but He
breathes His spirit into all of us.

I told all this to the interviewer at that press
conference. I told him that we were like all the
rest of men and women—two humans struggling, and looking hopefully toward heaven.

How I pity those Christians who put on the
false face of the spiritual snob! How I pity those
who fall into the trap of believing that they are
good, that they have it made, and that sin is forever behind them. This is just the moment when
the Adversary gets a good hold on our souls and
shakes the foundations of our faith in shattering experiences. Then it is that we realize (or
should realize) that we are not saints at all but
still blundering sinners very much in need of
instruction in the Way—that actually we are
still dragging our spiritual feet. Beware of thinking that you have heard everything and read
everything regarding your faith and that you
have no need of further instruction—*and con-
tinuing humility*. Beware of sitting smugly back
and waiting to be translated into heaven! That
is just plain stupid. Every day we live is a price-
less gift of God, loaded with possibilities to
learn something new, to gain fresh insights into
His great truths. To close our minds and hearts

is to reject the inner promptings of the Spirit—
to discover new dimensions of His truth.

In this autobiography, I am sure that I have
said some things with which some may not
agree; perhaps I should expect that. But I have
not written to please anybody or everybody—
that usually ends up in pleasing nobody! I have,
to the best of my ability, tried to set down here
an account of my personal experience before
and after Christ came into my life. I have
studied many religions, many different persuasions of thought in Christian belief, and I have
come, in this experience, to this: *the most important question in anyone's life is the question
asked by poor Pilate in Matthew 27:22:* "What
shall I do then with Jesus which is called
Christ?" No other question in the whole sweep
of human experience is as important as this.
It is the choice between life and death, between meaningless existence and life abundant.
What will *you* do with Christ? Accept Him and
live, or reject Him and die? *What else is there?*

His gifts are beyond reckoning, and He has
bestowed them upon us with a generous hand.
They are the fruits (benefits) of the Spirit. He
is the Tree; we are the branches, and as the
branches of an oak draw life from the trunk of
the tree, so when we draw upon His strength,
we find and produce rich fruits in our lives.
God is good in His benefits. I know, for He has
cushioned the hardest moments of my life, and
given me strength to go on. However hard the
way has been, I am at peace, forgetting that
which is behind, I press forward to the mark of

the high calling in Christ Jesus. I know I can trust Him.

I have been the woman at the well—and He has given me Living Water that has made fertile and meaningful the desert spots of my life.

Epilogue

In one way or another, in the past (that's in the "B.C.," or "Before Christ" came into my life), I think I tried to break nearly every one of the Ten Commandments in thought, word or deed.

I broke them to my sorrow. I have found that those Commandments *stand*, that they are irrevocable, and that those who attempt to break them break only themselves. We are wrong when we flatter ourselves in arrogance that we can break them. The reverse is true.

Jesus said, "Think not that I am come to destroy the law . . . , but to fulfil" (Matthew 5: 17). He died to give us eternal life, by allowing

Himself in His perfection, to be crucified as ransom for our failures to keep the Law—which includes the Commandments. I have no question whatever about this. I know in my heart, first-hand, that this is true, because it has worked out as plain gospel truth in my life.

Galatians 6:7–10 says, "Be not deceived; God is not mocked; for whatsoever a man soweth, that shall he also reap. For he that soweth to his flesh shall of the flesh reap corruption; but he that soweth to the Spirit shall of the Spirit reap life everlasting. And let us not be weary in well doing: for in due season we shall reap, if we faint not. As we have therefore opportunity, let us do good unto all men, especially unto them who are of the household of faith."

The illnesses, the tragedies of my life and the disillusionments have served as spiritual correction to my soul. They have shown me, beyond the shadow of a doubt, that in the flesh dwelleth no good thing, and that it is "the spirit that quickeneth; the flesh profiteth nothing" (John 6:63).

I am not bitter, nor questioning, toward God. I know better than to fall into that trap. Had I taken that attitude toward the semblance of tragedy that He has allowed in my Christian walk since the day He came into my heart and changed my life, I would not have learned a thing.

I do not say that God gave me German measles just before Robin was born, or that He led me to do something that would interrupt my pregnancy with her, causing her to be born

congenitally imperfect. I do not say that God
blew the tire on the church bus in the accident
that took Debbie's life. I do not say that God
inspired Sandy to drink that hard liquor in his
attempt to prove himself a man, and which
ended in his death. But I do believe that God
knew these things would happen, for He knows
our end, from the beginning of our lives. He
allowed those things to happen, knowing that
". . . all things work together for good to them
that love God and who are called according to
his purpose" (Romans 8:28). I am His child,
and He cares what happens to me and to those
all about me; His Word tells me that "The Lord
will perfect that which concerneth me" (Psalm
138:8). Robin, Debbie and Sandy are His children. He cared what happened to them.

Praise His Holy Name! He gave me heart
assurance that these three children of mine were
eternally safe in His keeping. Robin was an
infant when He took her, but she had been committed to His care. Debbie and Sandy had given
their lives to Christ. God gave me the blessed
assurance that Debbie was prayed up the day I
saw her walk to the altar (it was the day before
her death), rededicating her life to the Lord
only forty-eight hours after her twelfth birthday. She was radiant that day. Now, looking
back, I know that the light of God's smile was
already on Debbie's brow, and that He was preparing her for the journey. Sandy was known to
the men of his army company as "the guy who
always bowed his head and said grace at chow-
time, no matter who was looking." The letter

he wrote us one week before his death was eloquent witness to his faith in his Saviour and in his country.

God is a good God! The indescribable joy He has let me experience in the Spirit far transcends any trials He has let me experience. The joy He has given me in allowing me to work out my own salvation in fear and trembling— well, I wouldn't trade that for anything the world has to offer. The fact that He has permitted me to see each one of the children, and Roy, accept Jesus Christ means that He has been far more than fair with me. The tears He has allowed to dim the eyes of my flesh have cleared the eyes of my soul, bringing each time a new depth of spiritual understanding and vision—because I trust Him.

Yes, this woman at the well loves Him with her whole heart, and she is not ashamed to tell the world what He has done for her.

For I am not ashamed of the Gospel of Jesus Christ: for it is the power of God unto salvation to everyone that believeth (Romans 1:16).

For about ten seconds I stood there, my fingers curled around the deck of Luckies. Something crawled up my spine and made my teeth grind together, snapping off a sound that was a curse at the whole damn world. I knocked a drunk down getting around the corner of the bar and ripped the door open so the rain could lash at my face the way it had been wanting to. Behind me somebody yelled to shut the door.

I didn't have time to because I saw the guy halfway down the street, a vague silhouette under the overhead light, a dejected figure of a man too far gone to care anymore. But he was worth caring about to somebody in the Buick sedan that pulled away from the curb. The car slithered out into the light with a roar, and I heard the sharp cough of the gun over the slapping of my own feet on the sidewalk.

It only took two of them and the guy slammed forward on his face. The back door flew open and another shadow ran under the light, and from where I was I could see him bend over and frisk the guy with a blurred motion of his hands.

I should have waited, damn it. I shouldn't have tried a shot from where I was. A .45 isn't built for range and the slug ripped a groove in the pavement and screamed off down the block. The guy let out a startled yell and tore back toward the car with the other guy yelling for him to hurry. He damn near made it, then one of the ricochets took him through the legs and he went down with a scream.

Nobody but me had paid any attention to him. He threw a buck on the bar, had a shot, then brought the other shot over to his table. Still nobody paid any attention to him. Maybe they were used to seeing guys who could cry.

He set the drink down and took the coat off the bundle. It was quite a bundle, all right. It was a little kid about a year old who was sound asleep. I said something dirty to myself and felt my shoulders hunch up in disgust. The rain, the bar, a kid, and a guy who cried. It made me sicker than I was.

I couldn't take my eyes off the guy. He was only a little squirt who looked as if he had never had enough to eat. His clothes were damp and ragged, clinging to him like skin. He couldn't have been any older than me, but his face was seamed around the mouth and eyes and his shoulders hung limply. Whatever had been his purpose in life, he had given up long ago.

But damn it, he kept crying. I could see the tears running down his cheeks as he patted the kid and talked too low to be heard. His chest heaved with a sob and his hands went up to cover his face. When they came away he bent his head and kissed the kid on top of his head.

All of a sudden my drink tasted lousy.

I turned around to put a quarter in the cigarette machine so I wouldn't have to look at him again when I heard his chair kick back and saw him run to the door. This time he had nothing in his arms.

The other guy didn't wait. He jammed the gas down and wrenched the wheel over as hard as he could, and the guy shrieking his lungs out in the gutter forgot the pain in his legs long enough to let out one final, terrified yell before the wheels of the car made a pulpy mess of his body. My hand kept squeezing the trigger until there were only the flat echoes of the blasts that were drowned out by the noise of the car's exhaust and the futile gesture as the gun held opened, empty.

And there I was standing over a dead little guy who had two holes in his back and the dried steaks of tears on his face. He didn't look tired anymore. He seemed to be smiling. What was left of the one in the gutter was too sickening to look at.

I opened the cigarettes and stuck one in my mouth. I lit it and breathed out the smoke, watching it sift through the rain. The guy couldn't hear me, but I said, "It's a hell of a city, isn't it, feller?"

© 1951 by E.P. Dutton, a division of Penguin USA, Inc.

The Big Kill *is available in a special Fortieth Anniversary edition, along with five other classic Mickey Spillane novels featuring Mike Hammer. Ask for them at your local bookseller.*

MASTERS OF MYSTERY